D1563795

SIMPLE DEFINED BENEFIT PLANS: METHODS OF ACTUARIAL FUNDING

SIMPLE DEFINED BENEFIT PLANS: METHODS OF ACTUARIAL FUNDING

Elaine A. Scott, M.S.P.A., Enrolled Actuary

DOW JONES-IRWIN
Homewood, Illinois 60430

I dedicate this book to my husband, Ernest Scott, my father, Richard Anderson, and my son, Andy. Thanks for the encouragement.

This publication is designed to provide accurate and authoritative information in regard to the subject matter covered. It is sold with the understanding that neither the author nor the publisher is engaged in rendering legal, accounting, or other professional service. If legal advice or other expert assistance is required, the services of a competent professional person should be sought.

From a Declaration of Principles jointly adopted by a Committee of the American Bar Association and a Committee of Publishers.

Project editor: Karen J. Murphy
Production manager: Bette Ittersagen
Compositor: Weimer Typesetting Company, Inc.
Typeface: 11/13 Times Roman
Printer: Arcata Graphics/Kingsport

Library of Congress Cataloging-in-Publication Data
Scott, Elaine A.
   Simple defined benefit plans : methods of actuarial funding /
Elaine A. Scott.
     p.   cm.
   Includes index.
   ISBN 1-55623-119-9
   1. Defined benefit pension plans—Accounting.   2. Defined benefit pension plans—Mathematics.   3. Defined benefit pension plans—United States. I. Title.
HF5686.05S37   1989
657'.75—dc 19   88–34912
                                                              CIP

Printed in the United States of America
1 2 3 4 5 6 7 8 9 0 K 6 5 4 3 2 1 0 9

PREFACE

When I started my career in the pension business, and again when I was responsible for training new employees, I searched for a beginner's manual on defined benefit plan calculations. I wanted a text that minimized the use of actuarial symbols and instead stressed definitions and easy-to-understand formulas. Since I never found such a text, I decided to write one.

My goal is to reduce defined benefit calculations to simple definitions and simple math. I believe this text will be helpful to beginning actuarial students and beginning employees of pension administration and actuarial firms. In addition, this text could prove helpful to professionals in related fields, such as pension law and accounting.

Advanced pension law and actuarial math are not covered in full detail in this text. I kept the sample calculations simple in order to avoid confusing the basic concepts the beginner must learn.

I received a lot of encouragement and help while writing this text. I'd like to thank Lee Cottrill, my mentor, and the American Society of Pension Actuaries Education and Examination Committee for their interest and encouragement. I'd also like to thank Chris Moore, with Financial Data Planning, for her review. I'd like to thank my friend Jean Denyer for her help.

Elaine A. Scott, M.S.P.A., Enrolled Actuary

CONTENTS

APPENDIXES

PART 1

OVERVIEW

CHAPTER 1

OVERVIEW OF DEFINED
BENEFIT PLANS

WHAT IS A DEFINED BENEFIT PLAN?

A defined benefit plan is a type of pension plan. Pension plans provide retirement benefits for employees and are usually qualified under the requirements of the Internal Revenue Code. A qualified plan satisfies rules for eligibility, participation, benefits, vesting, and funding. While some pension plans are not qualified, for the purposes of this book, we will deal exclusively with qualified plans.

There are two basic types of pension plan: *defined benefit* and *defined contribution*. In a defined contribution plan, the annual contributions (or allocations) are defined in the plan document. Profit sharing, 401(k), target, and money purchase plans are all types of defined contribution pension plans. In a defined benefit plan, the benefits are specifically defined. A defined benefit plan usually covers retirement benefits, early retirement benefits, death and disability benefits, and benefits due upon termination.

A simple example of a retirement benefit that could be found in a defined benefit plan is as follows:

> The plan participant (eligible employee) shall be entitled to receive a monthly benefit equal to 50 percent of average monthly compensation. This benefit will begin at age 65 and will continue for the life of the participant. Compensation shall be averaged over the 5 year period ending at age 65.

WHY DO EMPLOYERS ADOPT DEFINED BENEFIT PLANS?

Many employers adopt defined benefit plans for their employees because the retirement benefits are known and are guaranteed. Guarantees are in the form of the minimum funding standards and the Pension Benefit Guaranty Corporation. Minimum funding standards will be discussed in detail in Chapter 11. The Pension Benefit Guaranty Corporation, a government agency, guarantees certain plan benefits in the case of plan termination. This agency is primarily funded through the collection of premiums from most sponsors of defined benefit plans. Many employees, especially those nearing retirement, appreciate the security of knowing what to expect when they retire.

In contrast, under a defined contribution plan, the participant cannot know what monthly benefit to expect at retirement because only the contributions are known. The actual benefits at retirement are based on the accumulation of the contributions plus investment earnings. If the investment earnings are great, that plan's participants will have higher benefits than if the investment earnings were poor. Also, if participants start in a defined contribution plan when they are young, participants will have more time to receive contributions and accumulate earnings in their accounts. In a defined benefit plan, if the investments are better than expected, the employer's contributions would be reduced; the benefits stay the same. In other words, under a defined benefit plan, the employer bears the risk on investment earnings; under defined contribution plans, the employee does. Funding will be discussed further in the next section.

Many small employers with an older, highly paid owner establish defined benefit plans for quick accumulation of funds for retirement and for the resulting large tax deductions. Other employers adopt defined benefit plans to compete with other employers' or union plans.

WHAT DOES IT MEAN TO FUND A DEFINED BENEFIT PLAN?

To fund a plan means to contribute to a trust fund so there will be enough money in the trust to pay benefits according to the plan document. There are three concepts of funding:

1. *Pay-as-you-go*. Contributions are made in an amount sufficient to pay the retirement benefits currently due retired employees. No contributions are made until there are retirees, and contributions are made for only current, not future, benefits. This concept cannot be used for qualified plans.

2. *Terminal funding*. Terminal funding is similar to pay-as-you-go, in that no contributions are made until there are retired employees. When an employee retires, a lump sum contribution is actuarially calculated in an amount sufficient to pay benefits for the rest of the participant's life. The participant's expected mortality and a postretirement interest rate are assumed. This concept also cannot be used for qualified plans.

3. *Prefunding*. All qualified plans use the prefunding concept. Contributions are calculated actuarially, usually annually, taking into consideration employees' future benefits, the trust fund's earnings, and employee turnover, mortality, and salary increases. The expected earnings (interest) rate, turnover, mortality, and salary increase rates are actuarial assumptions chosen by the plan's actuary.

Prefunding spreads the cost of providing retirement benefits over a number of years. Employers usually prefer this concept because cash flow from the employer to the plan is uniform and predictable. Prefunding allows for the accumulation of contributions with investment earnings, as discussed above. Therefore, contributions should be less with prefunding than under the pay-as-you-go method. Also, if the plan is qualified, the contributions are deductible, and the earnings tax-deferred.

Prefunding a defined benefit plan requires the use of a *funding method*. A funding method is a set procedure used to actuarially calculate the annual contributions to the plan. The Employee Retirement Income Security Act of 1974 specified certain allowable funding methods. In addition, there are allowable variations on the specified methods. To make things even more confusing, the same funding method often will be called two different names by two different actuaries. This book uses the traditional names for the funding methods, although these traditional names are not very descriptive. However, each funding method will be categorized in order to be compared and identified more easily.

WHAT DO I NEED TO KNOW IN ORDER TO UNDERSTAND FUNDING METHODS?

Although every effort was made to keep things simple, this book assumes the student has some knowledge in the following areas:

Simple algebra.

Financial (interest) calculations.

Actuarial notation.

Basic pension law.

There are many good texts available on these subjects. Additionally, the appendixes of this book contain quick reviews of financial calculations and actuarial notation.

The student should note that only the simplest actuarial assumptions were used in the examples. In Chapter 10, other assumptions and their effects on funding are discussed.

CHAPTER 2

OVERVIEW AND CATEGORIZATION OF FUNDING METHODS

As mentioned in Chapter 1, a funding method is a set procedure used to actuarially calculate the annual contributions to a defined benefit pension plan. The Employee Retirement Income Security Act of 1974 (ERISA) specified certain allowable funding methods. Some variations are allowed. The funding methods have certain similarities to and differences from each other. These similarities and differences are outlined in this chapter.

The procedures for contribution calculations are based on certain concepts. These concepts can be used to define and categorize each funding method. Each concept will be discussed separately, and a chart will follow showing which funding methods use which concepts. Chapters 3 through 8 will illustrate the specific calculations under each funding method.

PROJECTED BENEFIT COMPARED WITH ACCRUED BENEFIT METHODS

A projected retirement benefit is the benefit a participant can expect to receive under a defined benefit plan if the participant continues to work for the employer and continues to participate in the plan until normal retirement age. An accrued retirement benefit is the benefit a participant can expect to receive due to his or her service or plan participation completed to date. Usually, the accrued benefit is subject to vesting. The vested accrued benefit is nonforfeitable if the employee quits.

Both the retirement benefit and the accrued benefit are defined in the plan document. We saw an example of a retirement benefit in Chapter 1. An example of an accrued benefit definition follows:

> The accrued benefit will be a portion of the normal retirement benefit under the plan, calculated by multiplying the normal retirement benefit by a fraction, the numerator of which is the total service with the employer to date, and the denominator of which is the total possible service with the employer to normal retirement age.

Funding methods can base calculations on either projected or accrued retirement benefits. For funding methods based on projected retirement benefits, the annual contribution depends on projected retirement benefits. Funding methods based on accrued benefits use the accrued benefit in calculating the annual contribution. Most funding methods are based on projected retirement benefits.

Examples of the accrued benefit methods are the unit credit and the projected unit credit methods. However, the projected unit credit method is often considered to be a hybrid method, as will be discussed in Chapter 9. All other funding methods are projected benefit methods. The attained age normal method, also discussed in Chapter 9, can be considered a hybrid method but usually is considered a projected benefit method.

INDIVIDUAL COMPARED WITH
AGGREGATE METHODS

Contribution calculations can be done on an individual (participant-by-participant) basis or can be done in the aggregate for the entire plan. When individual-basis funding methods are used, contributions are calculated for each participant and are added to arrive at required plan contributions. When aggregate-basis funding methods are used, benefits are calculated on an individual basis, but contributions are calculated in the aggregate for the entire plan.

Examples of individual-basis funding methods are: individual level premium, entry age normal, unit credit, and individual spread gain methods. (Individual spread gain is also known as individual aggregate funding method, although individual spread gain is possibly the more descriptive and least confusing term.) Examples of aggregate-basis funding methods are: aggregate, frozen initial liability, and attained age normal funding methods.

IMMEDIATE GAIN COMPARED WITH SPREAD GAIN METHODS

A funding method can be categorized by whether an actuarial gain (or loss) is specifically recognized or whether the gain or loss is spread into the contribution calculations and is not recognized separately. To identify the differences between these types of funding methods, some terms must be introduced and defined.

Normal Cost
According to ERISA, normal cost is "the portion of the actuarial present value of benefits assigned to a particular year in respect of an individual participant or the plan as a whole. . . ." Since benefits are funded over a number of years, this term is given to the amount of benefits assigned to the year in question.

Actuarial (or Experience) Gain or Loss
The actuarial gain or loss is an amount arising each year when the actual plan facts do not coincide with the actuarial assumptions. For example, if the actuary assumes the trust will earn 6 percent and it actually earns 8 percent during the year, there will be an actuarial gain (assuming all other assumptions are met). If the actuary assumes five participants will terminate before becoming eligible to receive retirement benefits and two participants terminate, then there will be an actuarial loss (assuming again that all other assumptions are met). Actuarial gains or losses can be calculated by each individual source (i.e., interest earnings, employee turnover, salary increases, death, and so on), or they can be calculated as a net amount.

Under immediate gain funding methods, normal costs and an actuarial gain or loss are calculated separately each year. This gain (or loss) is amortized over a period of years. The amortization credit (or charge for a loss) is subtracted (or added) to the normal cost for the year. A separate record of these amortization amounts is kept until each is fully amortized.

Under spread gain funding methods, the actuarial gain or loss is not specifically calculated but causes variation in the normal cost amounts. The normal cost is adjusted automatically, taking the actuarial gain or loss into consideration over the expected future years of employees' plan participation.

Examples of immediate gain funding methods are the individual level premium, entry age normal, and unit credit funding methods. Examples of spread gain funding methods are the individual spread gain, aggregate, frozen initial liability, and attained age normal funding methods.

PAST SERVICE LIABILITY COMPARED WITH NO PAST SERVICE LIABILITY FUNDING METHODS

Most defined benefit plans are established after the employers started business. Therefore, there will often be employees who have had service with an employer before plan participation. Some funding methods separately recognize a cost due to employees' service before inception of the plan. These funding methods are categorized as funding methods with past service liability. Generally, to calculate a past service liability, we assume the plan had annual normal costs prior to when the plan actually started. The past service liability is the accumulation of the hypothetical normal costs, which in addition to future normal costs are sufficient to pay for all benefits if assumptions are realized. Another definition of past service liability is that it is the present value of benefits minus the present value of future normal costs at inception. Therefore, the past service liability can be calculated either retrospectively or prospectively. This past service liability is then amortized over a fixed number of years. The amortization payment is added to the normal cost to determine the required contribution to the plan. (If the method is also an immediate gain type, the amortizations for gains and losses must be added in also.)

Funding methods without past service liability do not separately recognize and amortize this cost. Costs due to employees' service before inception of the plan are part of the normal cost calculation.

TABLE 2–1
Categorization of Funding Methods

Type Funding Method	Projected/Accrued	Immediate/Spread Gain	Individual/Aggregate	Supplemental/No Supplemental Liability
Accrued benefit	A	—	—	S
Projected accrued benefit	Combination	—	—	S
Individual level premium	P	S	—	NS
Individual spread gain	P	—	—	NS
Entry age normal	P	S	A	S
Frozen initial liability	P	S	A	S
Aggregate	P	S	A	NS
Attained age normal	Combination	S	A	S

Examples of . . . the entry . . . are actuarial . . . and attained age normal. Examples of . . . the individual level premium, individual spread gain, and aggregate funding combinations . . .

The choice of an acceptable funding methods are important . . . conditions why . . . conditions are made under a certain funding . . .

FIGURE 2–1
Minimum Contributions

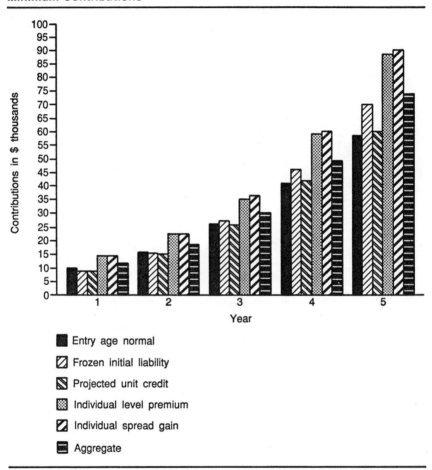

Examples of funding methods with past service liability are: entry age normal, frozen initial liability, unit credit, and attained age normal. Examples of funding methods without past service liability are: individual level premium, individual spread gain, and aggregate funding methods.

The concepts of categorizing funding methods are important to understanding why certain calculations are made under a certain funding method. These concepts will become clearer with the numerical examples in the subsequent chapters. Table 2–1 (see p. 11) summarizes the concepts used by each funding method as outlined in this chapter. Figure 2–1 compares the minimum required contributions for several funding methods, using data based in the following chapters.

PART 2

PROJECTED BENEFIT FUNDING METHODS

CHAPTER 3

INDIVIDUAL LEVEL PREMIUM FUNDING METHOD

The individual level premium funding method is a projected benefit, immediate gain, individual-basis funding method with no past service liability. This funding method, one of the simplest to explain, is rarely used. Traditionally, it has been used for very small defined benefit plans that are partially funded by life insurance. An insured plan typically has whole or universal life insurance policies as a portion of its investments. Insured plans will be discussed further in Chapter 9.

To more easily compare funding methods, the same data are used in most calculations. The data are listed at the beginning of each chapter.

PLAN AND INDIVIDUAL DATA USED IN ILLUSTRATIONS

Plan Information

Normal retirement benefit: 50 percent of final year compensation.

Normal retirement age: 65.

Accrual method: current/total possible service.

Assumed interest rate: 6 percent.

Postretirement mortality: UP84 Unisex.

Contribution made on first day of first plan year: $15,200.

Trust fund balance as of first day of second plan year: $16,000.

Contribution made on last day of second plan year: $23,000.

Trust fund balance as of first day of third plan year: $40,000.

Employee Information

Participant 1

Age at plan inception: 55.
Age at employment: 40.
Compensation plan year 1: $40,000.
Compensation plan year 2: $60,000.
Compensation plan year 3: $70,000.

Participant 2

Age at plan inception: 30.
Age at employment: 25.
Compensation plan year 1: $15,000.
Compensation plan year 2: $20,000.
Compensation plan year 3: $25,000.

Participant 3

Age at employment and plan participation: 35.
Compensation plan year 3: $10,000.

Other information to be used in the calculations include the annuity purchase rate derived from the interest and mortality assumptions and the applicable present value and annuity-certain factors obtained from the appendixes.

CALCULATIONS—THE FIRST PLAN YEAR

Since the individual level premium funding method is a projected benefit funding method, we must first calculate the projected benefit for each participant. For simplicity, we will assume the participant's final compensation will be the same as the participant's current compensation. (Salary scales will be discussed in Chapter 10.)

Participant 1

Monthly benefit = $40,000 × 0.050 / 12 = $1,667 (rounded).

Participant 2

Monthly benefit = $15,000 × 0.50 / 12 = $625.

Since the individual level premium funding method is an individual-based funding method, the normal cost is calculated separately for each participant. Chapter 2 defined normal cost as the portion of benefits assigned to the year. Since we are calculating the first year's contribution, there cannot be an actuarial gain or loss (as defined in Chapter 2) because there is no actual experience to compare against the actuarial assumptions. Therefore, for the first plan year, only a normal cost is calculated. Some new terms must be introduced and defined in order to calculate this normal cost:

Annuity Purchase Rate. The annuity purchase rate is an amount derived from the interest rate, postretirement mortality rate, and normal retirement age of the plan. This rate can be in various forms, including in actuarial notation. For this book, however, it will be stated as the number of dollars needed to buy an annuity of one dollar a month beginning at normal retirement age and continuing for the life of the participant. Given the interest rate and mortality table used in our examples, this amount is $115.21. The derivation of this amount is included in the appendixes.

Cash at Retirement. Cash at retirement refers to the total amount needed at normal retirement age to pay the normal retirement benefit under the plan. The cash at retirement amount is a lump sum that would be sufficient to pay retirement benefits in an annuity form. Simply, it is the projected monthly benefit calculated for the participant multiplied by the annuity purchase rate.

Under the individual level premium funding method, the normal cost is the level annual contribution that accumulates to the necessary cash at retirement. If the normal cost is contributed each year until a participant's retirement, and interest at exactly the assumed rate is earned, and assuming no other plan changes or deviations from plan assumptions, the cash at retirement will have accumulated. To determine this level annual contribution (normal cost), we must divide the cash at retirement by a factor. The factor used is known as *the accu-*

mulation of one dollar per year and is shown and defined in the appendixes. In actuarial notation, it is $\ddot{s}_{\overline{n}|i}$ (which is read s double-dot angle n at interest i, n = the number of years to retirement).

Participant 1
Since Participant 1 is now age 55, 10 years remain until the normal retirement age. The accumulation factor is 13.972. Therefore, the normal cost for Participant 1 is calculated as follows:

$1,667 × 115.21 = $192,055 Cash at retirement.
$192,055 / 13.972 = $13,746 Normal cost.

Participant 2
Participant 2 is now age 30, so 35 years remain until the normal retirement age. The accumulation factor is 118.121. Therefore, the normal cost for Participant 2 is calculated as follows:

$625 × 115.21 = $72,006 Cash at retirement.
$72,006 / 118.121 = $610 Normal cost.

Therefore, the total normal cost for the plan's first plan year is:

$13,746 + $610 = $14,356 Normal cost.

CALCULATIONS—THE SECOND PLAN YEAR

The calculations in the second year are complicated by two factors: the compensation increases and the actuarial gain or loss calculation. (Remember, the individual level premium funding method is an immediate gain funding method.) First, we must calculate the increase in the projected normal retirement benefit due to the compensation increases.

Participant 1

Monthly benefit = $60,000 × 0.50 / 12 = $2,500.
Additional monthly benefit = $2,500 − $1,667 = $833.

Participant 2

Monthly benefit = $20,000 × 0.50 / 12 = $833.
Additional monthly benefit = $833 − $625 = $208.

We now calculate the additional normal cost based on the additional monthly benefit. It is calculated in the same fashion as the original normal cost, but the accumulation factor used is for one less year.

Participant 1

Additional cash at retirement = \$833 × 115.21 = \$95,970.
Additional normal cost = \$95,970 / 12.181* = \$7,879.

* The accumulation factor is based on nine years to retirement.

Participant 2

Additional cash at retirement = \$208 × 115.21 = \$23,964.
Additional normal cost = \$23,964 / 110.435* = \$217.

* The accumulation factor is based on 34 years to retirement.

The total additional normal cost = \$7,879 + \$217 = \$8,096. Therefore, the total second year normal cost for the plan is the additional normal cost plus the original normal cost, \$14,356 + \$8,096 = \$22,452.

Every year an additional piece of normal cost is calculated and added to the previous year's normal cost. Keeping track of these pieces is a drawback to using this funding method.

We now must calculate the actuarial gain or loss that occurred during the first plan year. We need to introduce and define several terms before doing this calculation.

Present Value of Future Benefits.   The present value of future benefits is the cash at retirement for each participant multiplied by an appropriate present value factor. The factor is based on the interest rate and the number of years until the participant reaches normal retirement age. The present value factors are defined and listed in the appendixes. The actuarial symbol for this factor is v^n (v to the nth power, n = the number of years until retirement). The present value of future benefits is the value now of benefits to be paid at normal retirement age.

Present Value of Future Normal Costs.   The present value of future normal costs is the normal cost for each participant multiplied by a factor known as *the present value of one dollar per year*. This factor is based on the interest rate and the number of years until normal retirement age. These factors are defined and listed in the appendixes. The actuarial symbol for this factor is $\ddot{a}_{\overline{n}|i}$ (which is read a double-dot angle n, with interest rate i, n = number of years). In theory, the present value of future normal costs is the amount of future benefits that should be covered by future normal cost contributions.

Accrued Liability.   The accrued liability is the present value of future benefits minus the present value of future normal costs. In theory, the accrued liability is the accumulation of past normal cost contributions.

Unfunded Liability.   The unfunded liability is the accrued liability minus the trust assets.

Expected Unfunded Liability.   The expected unfunded liability is the unfunded liability that would be expected if all actuarial assumptions proved correct for the plan year. It is calculated as follows:

Prior unfunded liability + Prior normal cost
× Interest rate (in this example, 1.06) − Actual plan contributions
(increased by interest from the date of contribution to plan year end)
= Expected unfunded liability.

Actuarial Gain or Loss.   The actuarial gain or loss is the expected unfunded liability minus the actual unfunded liability. As defined in Chapter 2, the actuarial gain or loss is the amount arising each year when the actual plan facts do not coincide with the actuarial assumptions. (The actual unfunded liability for purposes of this calculation should be calculated before any change in plan benefit formula and assumptions. These changes are amortized separately.)

We will now calculate the amounts corresponding to these terms and determine the actuarial gain or loss that occurred during the first plan year.

Present Value of Benefits

Participant 1: $2,500 × 115.21 × .59190 = $170,482.
Participant 2: $833 × 115.21 × .13791 = $13,235.
Total = $183,717.

Present Value of Future Normal Costs

Participant 1: $21,625 × 7.210 = $155,916.
Participant 2: $827 × 15.230 = $12,595.
Total = $168,511.

Accrued Liability

$183,717 − $168,511 = $15,206.

Unfunded Liability

$15,206 − $16,000 = ($794).

According to Revenue Ruling 81-213, which describes rules for calculating experience gains or losses for minimum funding standards, an unfunded liability must be greater than or equal to zero, and therefore would be zero, instead of ($794). Minimum funding standards are discussed in Chapter 11.

Expected Unfunded Liability

Prior unfunded liability:	$ 0
Prior normal cost:	14,356
× 1.06	15,217
− (15,200 × 1.06 = 16,112)	$ (895).

Actuarial Gain or Loss

(895) − 0 = (895).

An amortization base would now be created to amortize this loss. Since it is a loss, the amortization base would increase the required minimum and legal maximum deductions as it is amortized over time.

In future years, the actuarial gains or losses are calculated the same way and then are amortized separately until considered fully amortized.

CALCULATIONS—THE THIRD PLAN YEAR

The third year's calculations are complicated by the compensation increases, the actuarial gain or loss, and the addition of a new employee. As in the first and second plan years, the first step is to calculate the monthly benefit. Then the additional cash at retirement and normal costs can be calculated.

Participant 1

$$\text{Monthly benefit} = \$70,000 \times 0.50 / 12 = \$2,917.$$
$$\text{Additional monthly benefit} = \$2,917 - 2,500 = \$417.$$
$$\text{Additional cash at retirement} = \$417 \times 115.21 = \$48,043.$$
$$\text{Additional normal cost} = \$48,043 / 10.491 = \$4,579.$$
$$\text{Total normal cost} = \$13,746 + 7,879 + 4,579$$
$$= \$26,204.$$

(The accumulation of one dollar per year factor was for eight years.)

Participant 2

$$\text{Monthly benefit} = \$25,000 \times 0.50 / 12 = \$1,042.$$
$$\text{Additional monthly benefit} = \$1,042 - 833 = \$209.$$
$$\text{Additional cash at retirement} = \$209 \times 115.21 = \$24,079.$$
$$\text{Additional normal cost} = \$24,079 / 103.184 = \$233.$$
$$\text{Total normal cost} = \$610 + 217 + 233 = \$1,060.$$

(The accumulation of one dollar per year factor was for 33 years.)

Participant 3 (the New Employee)

$$\text{Monthly benefit} = \$10,000 \times 0.50 / 12 = \$417.$$
$$\text{Cash at retirement} = \$417 \times 115.21 = \$48,043.$$
$$\text{Normal cost} = \$48,043 / 83.802 = \$573.$$

(The accumulation of one dollar per year factor was for 30 years.)

Note that since Participant 3 was new, there is only one piece of normal cost. The total normal cost for the third year is: $26,204 + 1,060 + 573 = $27,837.

Now the actuarial gain or loss can be calculated for the third plan year. The process is the same as for the second plan year. Recall that the actuarial gain or loss is the expected unfunded liability minus the actual unfunded liability. As before, the following equations are used.

$$\text{Unfunded liability} = \text{Accrued liability} - \text{Trust assets.}$$

$$\text{Accrued liability} = \text{Present value of future benefits} - \text{Present value future normal costs.}$$

Expected unfunded liability = (Prior unfunded liability + Prior normal cost) × 1.06 − (Plan contributions increased by interest from the date of contribution to plan year end).

The calculations are as follows:

Present Value of Future Benefits

Participant 1: $2,917 × 115.21 × .62741 = $210,852.
Participant 2: $1,042 × 115.21 × .14619 = $17,550.
Participant 3: $417 × 115.21 × .17411 = $8,365.
Total = $236,767.

Remember that the present value of future benefits is the value now of the benefits that will be received at normal retirement age. The present value of one dollar table in the appendixes was used for these calculations.

Present Value of Future Normal Costs

Participant 1: $26,204 × 6.582 = $172,475.
Participant 2: $1,060 × 15.084 = $15,989.
Participant 3: $573 × 14.591 = $8,361.
Total = $196,825.

Remember that the present value of future normal costs is the value now of the normal costs amounts to be deposited in the future. The present value of one dollar per year factors are used.

Accrued Liability

$236,767 − 196,825 = $39,942.

Unfunded Liability

$39,942 − 40,000 = $(58) = 0 (due to Revenue Ruling 81-213).

Expected Unfunded Liability

Prior unfunded liability:	$ 0
Prior normal cost:	22,452
× 1.06	23,799
− Contribution	23,000
=	$ 799.

Actuarial Gain or Loss

$$799 - 0.00 = \$799.$$

The $799 gain is then amortized over a period of years to determine the actual contribution to the plan for the third plan year. Because it is a gain, meaning there is more money than expected, the amortization amount is subtracted from the sum of the normal cost and the previous loss amortization.

The following set of study problems is designed to reinforce what was covered in Chapters 1 through 3.

STUDY PROBLEMS

1. Why is the annuity purchase rate the same for both participants?

2. When would annuity purchase rates differ for different participants?

3. Why is there no past service liability in the individual level premium funding method?

4. Calculate the normal cost for the following employee, using the same specifications as in the example.

Participant 4:

Age at plan participation: 45.
Age at employment: 44.
Compensation: $32,000.

CHAPTER 4

ENTRY AGE NORMAL FUNDING METHOD

The entry age normal funding method is a projected benefit, immediate gain, individual-basis funding method with a past service liability. Therefore, the only difference between this funding method and the individual level premium funding method, discussed in Chapter 3, is the use of a past service liability. Unlike the individual level premium funding method, the entry age normal funding method is used frequently by both large and small plans.

The entry age normal funding method is widely used because it allows flexibility in making contributions. An employer can choose the amount of the contribution to be made as long as it falls within the calculated allowable range. Therefore, an employer can make the minimum required contribution in a lean year or the maximum deductible contribution in a good year.

Small plan sponsors must be careful when using the entry age normal funding method. A small plan can be in danger of underfunding if the minimum allowable contribution is usually made. This danger is especially possible if the highly paid participants are close to retirement when the plan begins.

The entry age normal funding method calculations will be illustrated using the following data.

PLAN AND INDIVIDUAL DATA USED
IN ILLUSTRATIONS

Plan Information

Normal retirement benefit: 50 percent of final year compensation.

Normal retirement age: 65.

Accrual method: current/total possible service.

Assumed interest rate: 6 percent.

Postretirement mortality: UP84 Unisex.

Contribution made on first day of first plan year: $15,200.

Trust fund balance as of first day of second plan year: $16,000.

Contribution made on last day of second plan year: $28,000.

Trust fund balance as of first day of third plan year: $45,000.

Employee Information

Participant 1

Age at plan inception: 55.

Age at employment: 40.

Compensation plan year 1: $40,000.

Compensation plan year 2: $60,000.

Compensation plan year 3: $70,000.

Participant 2

Age at plan inception: 30.

Age at employment: 25.

Compensation plan year 1: $15,000.

Compensation plan year 2: $20,000.

Compensation plan year 3: $25,000.

Participant 3

Age at employment and plan participation: 35.

Compensation plan year 3: $10,000.

Other information to be used in the calculations includes the annuity purchase rate derived from the interest and mortality assumptions and the applicable present value and annuity-certain factors obtained from the appendixes.

CALCULATIONS—THE FIRST PLAN YEAR

Since the entry age normal funding method is a projected benefit funding method, we calculate the projected benefit for each participant as we did in Chapter 3:

Participant 1

Monthly benefit = $40,000 × 0.50 / 12 = $1,667.

Participant 2

Monthly benefit = $15,000 × 0.50 / 12 = $625.

Since the entry age normal funding method is an individual-based funding method, the normal cost is calculated separately for each participant. The normal cost under this funding method is similar to the normal cost under the individual level premium funding method. The difference is that the normal cost is calculated from the participant's employment age instead of the participant's date of participation.

Participant 1

Since Participant 1 was 40 at the employment date, 25 years remain until normal retirement age. The accumulation factor (accumulation of one dollar per year) is 58.156. Therefore, the normal cost for Participant 1 is calculated as follows:

$1,667 × 115.21 (annuity purchase rate) = $192,055
= Cash at retirement.
$192,055 / 58.156 = $3,302 normal cost.

Participant 2

Since Participant 2 was age 25 at the employment date, there are 40 years until normal retirement age. The accumulation factor (accumulation of one dollar per year) is 164.048. The normal cost for Participant 2 is calculated as follows:

625×115.21 (annuity purchase rate) $= \$72,006$
$= $ Cash at retirement.
$\$72,006 \ / \ 164.048 = \$439$ normal cost.

Therefore, the total normal cost for the plan's first year is:

$$\$3,302 + \$439 = \$3,741 \text{ normal cost.}$$

Past Service Liability Calculation

The past service liability must be calculated for the entry age normal funding method first year calculations. The past service liability is the amount that could have been in the plan at plan inception if the plan would have been in existence on each participant's employment date.

The amount can be calculated in two ways when no salary scale assumption is used. The most straightforward method of calculation is to accumulate the calculated normal cost for the number of years between date of employment and date of plan inception. To illustrate:

Participant 1

$$\$3,302 \times 24.673 = \$81,470.$$

(The accumulation factor for 15 years is 24.673, using the accumulation of one dollar per year table.)

Participant 2

$$\$439 \times 5.975 = \$2,623.$$

(The accumulation factor for five years is 5.9750, using the accumulation of one dollar per year table.) Therefore, the total past service liability is $\$81,470 + 2,623 = \$84,093$.

The other way to calculate the past service liability is to use this formula:

Present value of benefits $-$ Present value of future normal costs
$= $ Past service liability.

Recall that this is the formula for accrued liability defined in Chapter 3. The past service liability calculation under this formula is a study problem at the end of this chapter.

The past service liability must be amortized over a period of 10 to 30 years, 40 years for pre-1974 plans. The amortization over 10 years using the present value of one dollar per year factor is: $84,093 / 7.802 = $10,778. The amortization over 30 years is: $84,093 / 14.591 = $5,763.

Therefore, the maximum contribution is: $10,778 + 3,741 = $14,519, and the minimum contribution is: $5,763 + 3,741 = $9,504.

CALCULATIONS—THE SECOND PLAN YEAR

Since the entry age normal funding method is an immediate gain method, the second year calculations are complicated by the actuarial gain or loss calculation. However, first we must recalculate the normal cost because of the increase in salaries. Unlike the individual level premium funding method, we do not need to keep track of the prior years' normal costs and calculate a separate additional normal cost to add to it.

Participant 1

Monthly benefit = $60,000 × 0.50 / 12 = $2,500.
Cash at retirement = $2,500 × 115.21 = $288,025.
Normal cost = $288,025 / 58.156 = $4,953.

Participant 2

Monthly benefit = $20,000 × 0.50 / 12 = $833.
Cost at retirement = $833 × 115.21 = $95,970.
Normal cost = $95,970 / 164.048 = $585.

The total normal cost for the second plan year is:

$4,953 + 585 = $5,538.

We now must calculate the actuarial gain or loss that occurred during the first plan year. This actuarial gain or loss is calculated in the same manner as it was calculated in Chapter 3. The formula for actuarial gain or loss is the expected unfunded liability minus the actual unfunded liability. As before, we must calculate the components to this equation.

Step 1: Calculate the present value of future benefits. This amount is the same as in Chapter 3. (The present value of one dollar factors are used.)

$$\text{Participant 1: } \$2,500 \times 115.21 \times .59190 = \$170,482.$$
$$\text{Participant 2: } \$833 \times 115.21 \times .13791 = \$13,235.$$
$$\text{Total} = \$183,717.$$

Step 2: Calculate the present value of future normal cost. This is calculated as in Chapter 3, except that the normal costs calculated under the entry age normal funding method are used. (The present value of one dollar per year factors are used.)

$$\text{Participant 1: } \$4,953 \times 7.210 = \$35,711.$$
$$\text{Participant 2: } \$585 \times 15.230 = \$8,910.$$
$$\text{Total} = \$44,621.$$

Step 3: Calculate accrued liability = Present value of future benefits − Present value of future normal costs.

$$\$183,717 - 44,621 = \$139,096.$$

Step 4: Calculate unfunded accrued liability = Accrued liability − Assets.

$$\$139,096 - 16,000 = \$123,096.$$

Step 5: Calculate expected unfunded liability.

Prior unfunded liability:	$84,093
Prior normal cost:	3,741
	$87,834

$87,834 × 1.06 =	$93,104
− (15,200 × 1.06)	− 16,112
	$76,992.

Step 6: Calculate experience gain or loss = Expected unfunded liability − Actual unfunded liability.

$$\$76,992 - 123,096 = (46,104).$$

This actuarial loss must be amortized over five years for minimum funding standards (discussed in Chapter 11). The amortization amount must be added to the normal cost and past service liability amortization to determine the required contribution. Using the present value of one dollar per year factors:

Amortization over 5 years = $46,104 / 4.465 = $10,326.

The actuarial loss can be amortized over 10 years for maximum deductions (discussed in Chapter 12).

Amortization over 10 years = $46,104 / 7.802 = $5,909.

Second year maximum contribution: $5,538 + 5,909 + 10,778 = $22,225. The second year minimum contribution is: $5,538 + 10,326 + 5,763 = $21,627.

CALCULATIONS—THE THIRD PLAN YEAR

The third plan year's calculations are complicated by the compensation increases, the actuarial gain or loss, and the addition of a new employee. As in the first and second plan years, the first step is to calculate the monthly benefit. Then a new normal cost can be calculated.

Participant 1

Monthly benefit = $70,000 × 0.50 / 12 = $2,917.
Cash at retirement = $2,917 × 115.21 = $336,068.
Normal cost = $336,068 / 58.156 = $5,779.

Participant 2

Monthly benefit = $25,000 × 0.50 / 12 = $1,042.
Cash at retirement = $1,042 × 115.21 = $120,049.
Normal cost = $120,049 / 164.048 = $732.

Participant 3

Monthly benefit = $10,000 × 0.50 / 12 = $417.
Cash at retirement = $417 × 115.21 = $48,043.
Normal cost = $48,043 / 83.802 = $573.

The total normal cost for the third year is: $5,779 + 732 + 573 = $7,084.

Now the actuarial gain or loss can be calculated for the third plan year. The process is the same as for the second plan year. As before, the actuarial gain or loss is the expected unfunded liability minus the actual unfunded liability. Calculating the components of this equation, we have:

Present Value of Future Benefits

Participant 1: $\$2,917 \times 115.21 \times .62741 = \$210,852.$
Participant 2: $\$1,042 \times 115.21 \times .14619 = \$17,550.$
Participant 3: $\$417 \times 115.21 \times .17411 = \$8,365.$
Total $= \$236,767.$

The present value of one dollar factors were used.

Present Value of Future Normal Costs

Participant 1: $\$5,779 \times 6.582 = \$38,037.$
Participant 2: $\$732 \times 15.084 = \$11,041.$
Participant 3: $\$573 \times 14.591 = \$8,361.$
Total $= \$57,439.$

The present value of one dollar per year factors were used.

Accrued Liability

Accrued liability = Present value of future benefits − Present value of future normal cost
= $\$236,767 - 57,439$
= $\$179,328.$

Unfunded Liability

Unfunded liability = Accrued liability − Trust assets
= $\$179,328 - 45,000$
= $\$134,328.$

Expected Unfunded Liability

Prior unfunded liability:	$123,096
Prior normal cost:	5,538
× 1.06	136,352
− Contribution	28,000
=	$108,352.

Actuarial Gain or Loss

$108,352 - 134,328 = \$(25,976).$

The loss is then amortized to determine the total contribution to the plan for the third plan year. Because it is a loss, the amortization amount is added to the normal cost and previous amortization amounts. Using the present value of one dollar per year factors, we can calculate 5-year and 10-year amortization amounts for the loss.

5-year amortization = $25,976 / 4.465 = $5,818.
10-year amortization = $25,976 / 7.802 = $3,329.

The third year maximum contribution would be: $7,084 (normal cost) + 10,778 (past service liability) + 5,909 (first loss) + 3,329 (second loss) = $27,100. However, the third year minimum contribution would be: $7,084 + 5,763 + 10,326 + 5,818 = $28,991. Since the minimum is higher, it is the maximum as well.

If there had been an actuarial gain, it would have been subtracted rather than added in the above minimum and maximum contribution calculations. Future years would be done similarly, adding or subtracting amortization amounts until each are fully amortized.

The following set of study problems is designed to reinforce what was covered in this chapter.

STUDY PROBLEMS

1. Calculate the first year past service liability under the second method.

2. Under the individual level premium funding method second year calculations, an additional normal cost is added to the original normal cost. Why is it unnecessary to perform this step under the entry age normal funding method?

3. Calculate the normal cost under the entry age normal funding method for the following employee, using the same specifications as in the example.

Participant 4

Age at plan participation: 44.
Age at employment: 45.
Compensation: $32,000.

4. Would you recommend the use of entry age normal funding method for our sample plan? Why or why not?

CHAPTER 5

INDIVIDUAL SPREAD GAIN FUNDING METHOD

The individual spread gain funding method is a projected benefit, spread gain, individual-basis funding method with no past service liability. It is often considered to be the simplest funding method, and therefore is widely used for small plans.

The same data are used in the individual spread gain funding method calculations as were used in previous chapters. One additional piece of data is included. The data follow:

PLAN AND INDIVIDUAL DATA USED IN ILLUSTRATIONS

Plan Information

Normal retirement benefit: 50 percent of final year compensation.

Normal retirement age: 65.

Accrual method: current/total possible service.

Assumed interest rate: 6 percent.

Postretirement mortality: UP84 Unisex.

Contribution made on first day of first plan year: $15,200.

Trust fund balance as of first day of second plan year: $16,000.

Schedule B credit balance on last day of first plan year: $896.

Contribution made on last day of second plan year: $23,000.

Trust fund balance as of first day of third plan year: $40,000.

Schedule B credit balance on last day of second plan year: $1,013.

Employee Information

Participant 1

Age at plan inception: 55.
Age at employment: 40.
Compensation plan year 1: $40,000.
Compensation plan year 2: $60,000.
Compensation plan year 3: $70,000.

Participant 2

Age at plan inception: 30.
Age at employment: 25.
Compensation plan year 1: $15,000.
Compensation plan year 2: $20,000.
Compensation plan year 3: $25,000.

Participant 3

Age at employment and plan participation: 35.
Compensation plan year 3: $10,000.

Other information that will be used in the calculations include the annuity purchase rate derived from the interest and mortality assumptions, and the applicable present value and annuity-certain factors obtained from the appendixes.

CALCULATIONS—THE FIRST PLAN YEAR

Since the individual spread gain funding method is a projected benefit funding method, we must first calculate the projected benefit for each participant. For purposes of simplicity, we again assume the participant's final compensation is the same as the participant's current compensation.

Participant 1

Monthly benefit = $40,000 × 0.50 / 12 = $1,667.

Participant 2

Monthly benefit = $15,000 × 0.50 / 12 = $625.

Since the individual spread gain funding method is an individual-based funding method, the normal cost is calculated separately for each participant. The normal cost is calculated using these steps (definitions follow):

Step 1: Present value of future benefits − Allocated assets = Present value of future normal cost.

Step 2: Present value of future normal cost / Present value of one dollar per year factor = Normal cost.

Present value of future benefits is the value now of retirement benefits to be received in the future. As in Chapter 3 and 4, this value is calculated by multiplying the cash value at retirement by the present value of one dollar factor.

Allocated assets is the portion of the trust assets allocated to each participant for calculation of the present value of future normal cost. This is not the same as an account balance under a defined contribution plan and is meaningful only in the context of the calculations. There are several ways to allocate the assets if you switch to individual aggregate from another funding method, but the most acceptable way is illustrated in the second plan year calculations. The illustrated way is used in all other cases.

Under the individual spread gain funding method, the present value of future normal cost is dependent on the present value of future benefits and the trust assets. Unlike under the individual level premium and entry age normal funding methods, it is calculated before the normal cost calculation.

Normal cost is again the annual amount to be contributed each year to the plan. However, under the individual spread gain funding method, it is dependent on the present value of future normal costs calculated under the above formula.

The present value factors used are determined for the number of years between the time of calculations and the participant's retirement date.

Since there are no assets at plan inception, the allocated assets for the first year is zero for both participants.

Participant 1

$$\text{Cash value at retirement} = \$1{,}667 \times 115.21$$
$$= \$192{,}055.$$
$$\text{Present value of benefits} = \$192{,}055 \times 0.55839$$
$$= \$107{,}242.$$
$$\text{Present value of future normal costs} = \$107{,}242 - 0$$
$$= \$107{,}242.$$
$$\text{Normal cost} = \$107{,}242 \, / \, 7.802$$
$$= \$13{,}745.$$

(The present value of one dollar per year factor for 10 years is 7.802.)

Participant 2

$$\text{Cash value at retirement} = \$625 \times 115.21$$
$$= \$72{,}006.$$
$$\text{Present value of benefits} = \$72{,}006 \times 0.13011$$
$$= \$9{,}369.$$
$$\text{Present value of future normal costs} = \$9{,}369 - 0$$
$$= \$9{,}369.$$
$$\text{Normal cost} = \$9{,}369 \, / \, 15.368$$
$$= \$610.$$

(The present value of one dollar per year factor for 35 years is 15.368.)
The total first year normal cost is:

$$\$13{,}745 + 610 = \$14{,}355.$$

CALCULATIONS—THE SECOND PLAN YEAR

The second year calculations are the same as the first. However, the plan assets must be allocated between the participants. Before the assets are allocated to each participant, the credit balance from the prior Schedule B must be subtracted. See Chapter 11 for the explanation of the minimum funding standard account credit balance.

The amounts to be used are given at the beginning of this chapter. However, for maximum deductibility purposes, prior nondeducted contributions are subtracted from the assets instead of the credit balance. Also, other adjustments to assets could be needed in cases of terminated or retired participants, unamortized bases for waivers of minimum funding, switchback from the alternative minimum funding account, and shortfall gains or losses. To keep our example simple, assume the credit balance is the correct amount to subtract. (Again, items pertaining to minimum funding are discussed further in Chapter 11.)

Assets are allocated in proportion to the prior year allocated assets plus prior year normal cost. Using this method, the allocation of assets would be as follows:

Participant 1

   $((13,745 + 0) / (14,355 + 0)) \times (16,000 - 896) = \$14,462.$

Participant 2

   $(($610 + 0) / (14,355 + 0)) \times 15,104 = \$642.$

The benefits are recalculated for the salary increase. As in prior chapters, Participant 1 = $2,500 and Participant 2 = $833. Factors for Participant 1 are based on 9 years until retirement. Factors for Participant 2 are based on 34 years until retirement.

The second year normal cost calculations for each participant follow:

Participant 1

$$
\begin{aligned}
\text{Cash at retirement} &= \$2,500 \times 115.21 \\
&= \$288,025. \\
\text{Present value of future benefits} &= \$288,025 \times 0.5919 \\
&= \$170,482. \\
\text{Present value of future normal costs} &= \$170,482 - 14,462 \\
&= \$156,020. \\
\text{Normal cost} &= \$156,020 / 7.21 \\
&= \$21,639.
\end{aligned}
$$

Participant 2

$$
\begin{aligned}
\text{Cash at retirement} &= \$833 \times 115.21 \\
&= \$95,970. \\
\text{Present value of future benefits} &= \$95,970 \times 0.13791 \\
&= \$13,235. \\
\text{Present value of future normal costs} &= \$13,235 - 642 \\
&= \$12,593. \\
\text{Normal cost} &= \$12,593 / 15.23 \\
&= \$827.
\end{aligned}
$$

Total normal cost for the second year is $21,639 + 827 = $22,466.

CALCULATIONS—THE THIRD PLAN YEAR

The third year calculations are the same as the first two years, with the addition of the new employee. Present value factors are based on 8 years for Participant 1, 33 years for Participant 2, and 30 years for Participant 3.

Again we allocate the assets minus the credit balance, $40,000 − 1,013 = $38,987, in proportion to the prior year allocated assets plus prior year normal cost. Because Participant 3 did not participate in the prior year, allocated assets are zero. The calculation of allocated assets for Participant 1 and 2 follow:

Participant 1

$$((\$14,462 + 21,639) / (15,104 + 22,466)) \times 38,987 = \$37,463.$$

Participant 2

$$((\$642 + 827) / (15,104 + 22,466)) \times 38,987 = \$1,524.$$

The third year normal cost calculations for each participant follow:

Participant 1

$$
\begin{aligned}
\text{Monthly benefit} &= \$70,000 \times 0.50 / 12 \\
&= \$2,917. \\
\text{Cash at retirement} &= \$2,917 \times 115.21 \\
&= \$336,068. \\
\text{Present value of future benefits} &= \$336,068 \times .62741 \\
&= \$210,852. \\
\text{Present value of future normal costs} &= \$210,852 - 37,463 \\
&= \$173,389. \\
\text{Normal cost} &= \$173,389 / 6.582 \\
&= \$26,343.
\end{aligned}
$$

Participant 2

$$
\begin{aligned}
\text{Monthly benefit} &= \$25,000 \times 0.50 / 12 \\
&= \$1,042. \\
\text{Cash at retirement} &= \$1,042 \times 115.21 \\
&= \$120,049.
\end{aligned}
$$

$$\text{Present value of future benefits} = \$120{,}049 \times .14619$$
$$= \$17{,}550.$$
$$\text{Present value of future normal costs} = \$17{,}550 - 1{,}524$$
$$= \$16{,}026.$$
$$\text{Normal cost} = \$16{,}026 / 15.084$$
$$= \$1{,}062.$$

Participant 3

$$\text{Monthly benefit} = \$10{,}000 \times 0.50 / 12$$
$$= \$417.$$
$$\text{Cash at retirement} = \$417 \times 115.21$$
$$= \$48{,}043.$$
$$\text{Present value of future benefits} = \$48{,}043 \times .17411$$
$$= \$8{,}365.$$
$$\text{Present value of future normal costs} = \$8{,}365 - 0$$
$$= \$8{,}365.$$
$$\text{Normal cost} = \$8{,}365 / 14.591$$
$$= \$573.$$

The third year total normal cost is $\$26{,}343 + 1{,}062 + 573 = \$27{,}978$.

STUDY PROBLEMS

1. Why is the first year normal cost the same under the individual spread gain as under the individual level premium?

2. As you will recall, under the individual level premium funding method, the formula for accrued liability was present value of benefits minus present value of future normal costs. If you were to use the same formula with individual spread gain funding method values, the accrued liability would be the same as what other figure? What would the unfunded liability always be?

3. What is the significance of the result of Problem 2 in regard to actuarial gains and losses?

CHAPTER 6

AGGREGATE FUNDING
METHOD

The aggregate funding method is a projected benefit, spread gain, aggregate-basis funding method with no past service liability. It is one of the simplest funding methods and therefore is widely used. It can be used for all sizes of plans. However, small plans with skewed participant age groups should carefully monitor a plan using aggregate funding method to insure adequate funding.

To illustrate the calculations under the aggregate funding method, the following data will be used.

PLAN AND INDIVIDUAL DATA USED
IN ILLUSTRATIONS

Plan Information

Normal retirement benefit: 50 percent of final year compensation.

Normal retirement age: 65.

Accrual method: current/total possible service.

Assumed interest rate: 6 percent.

Postretirement mortality: UP84 Unisex.

Contribution made on first day of first plan year: $12,000.

Trust fund balance as of first day of second plan year: $13,000.

Schedule B credit balance at end of first year: $191.

Contribution made on last day of second plan year: $19,640.

Trust fund balance as of first day of third plan year: $33,000.

Schedule B credit balance at end of second year: $182.

Employee Information

Participant 1

Age at plan inception: 55.
Age at employment: 40.
Compensation plan year 1: $40,000.
Compensation plan year 2: $60,000.
Compensation plan year 3: $70,000.

Participant 2

Age at plan inception: 30.
Age at employment: 25.
Compensation plan year 1: $15,000.
Compensation plan year 2: $20,000.
Compensation plan year 3: $25,000.

Participant 3

Age at employment and plan participation: 35.
Compensation plan year 3: $10,000.

Other information used in the calculations include the annuity purchase rate derived from the interest and mortality assumptions (115.21, as in previous chapters) and the applicable present value and annuity-certain factors obtained from the appendixes.

CALCULATIONS—THE FIRST PLAN YEAR

As in all projected benefit funding methods, we must first calculate the projected benefit for each participant. We will assume the participant's final compensation will be the same as the participant's current compensation. As before:

Participant 1

Monthly benefit = $40,000 \times 0.50 / 12 = $1,667$.

Participant 2

Monthly benefit = $15,000 \times 0.50 / 12 = 625.

Since the aggregate funding method is an aggregate-basis funding method, we do not separately calculate a normal cost for each participant. We do, however, calculate several items to be used in the normal cost calculations. These items are:

Present Value of Future Benefits.   As in the previously discussed funding methods, the present value of future benefits is calculated by multiplying the projected monthly benefit times the annuity purchase rate times the appropriate present value of one dollar factor from the appendixes.

Present Value of Future Salaries.   Each participant's salary is multiplied by the appropriate present value of one dollar per year factor from the appendixes. The present value of future salaries is the value now of all annual salaries that will be received from the calculation date until normal retirement age.

Using the data given, the calculations are as follows:

Present Value of Benefits

Participant 1: $1,667 × 115.21 × 0.55839 = $107,242.
Participant 2: $625 × 115.21 × 0.13011 = $9,369.
Total: $116,611.

Present Value of Future Salaries

Participant 1: $40,000 × 7.802 = $312,080.
Participant 2: $15,000 × 15.368 = $230,520.
Total: $542,600.

The next step is to determine the average temporary annuity factor by dividing the present value of future salaries by total compensation. The average temporary annuity is an average of the present value of one dollar per year factors for all participants, weighted by the salaries.

Average temporary annuity = $542,600 / $55,000 = 9.8655.

To determine the normal cost, we divide the present value of benefits by the average temporary annuity factor.

Normal cost = $116,611 / 9.8655 = $11,820.

CALCULATIONS—THE SECOND PLAN YEAR

The only difference between the first year and second year calculations under the aggregate funding method is that the trust assets must be considered. The trust assets are subtracted from the present value of benefits before the division by the average temporary annuity. But first, any credit balance determined in the minimum funding standard account (see Chapter 11) must be subtracted from the assets before applying the formula. For this plan year, our credit balance is $191.

As under the individual spread gain funding method, nondeducted contributions are subtracted instead of the credit balance when calculating the adjusted assets for maximum deductible contribution purposes. Also, there could be other assets adjustments in the case of terminated and retired participants, unamortized bases for minimum funding standard waivers, switchback from the alternative minimum funding standard account, and shortfall gains or losses. Minimum funding standards are discussed further in Chapter 11.

The calculations for the second year are as follows, starting with the recalculation of monthly benefits due to the salary increases:

Participant 1

Monthly benefit = $60,000 × 0.50 / 12 = $2,500.

Participant 2

Monthly benefit = $20,000 × 0.50 / 12 = $833.

Present Value of Benefits

Participant 1: $2,500 × 115.21 × 0.59190 = $170,482.
Participant 2: $833 × 115.21 × 0.13791 = $13,235.
Total: $183,717.

Present Value of Future Salaries

Participant 1: $60,000 × 7.210 = $432,600.
Participant 2: $20,000 × 15.230 = $304,600.
Total: $737,200.

Average Temporary Annuity

$$\$737,200 / \$80,000 = 9.215.$$

Normal Cost

$$(\$183,717 - (13,000 - 191)) / 9.215 = \$18,547.$$

CALCULATIONS—THE THIRD PLAN YEAR

The third plan year calculations are complicated by the addition of a new employee. However, the same procedure as before is used. First, the monthly benefits are recalculated for each participant due to the salary increases. We also calculate the present value of future benefits and the present value of future salary amounts for each participant using the appropriate present value factors.

Participant 1

$$\text{Monthly benefit} = \$70,000 \times 0.50 / 12 = \$2,917.$$
$$\text{Present value of future benefits} = \$2,917 \times 115.21 \times .62741$$
$$= \$210,852.$$
$$\text{Present value of future salary} = \$70,000 \times 6.582 = \$460,740.$$

Participant 2

$$\text{Monthly benefit} = \$25,000 \times 0.50 / 12 = \$1,042.$$
$$\text{Present value of future benefits} = \$1,042 \times 115.21 \times .14619$$
$$= \$17,550.$$
$$\text{Present value of future salary} = \$25,000 \times 15.084 = \$377,100.$$

Participant 3

$$\text{Monthly benefit} = \$10,000 \times 0.50 / 12 = \$417.$$
$$\text{Present value of future benefits} = \$417 \times 115.21 \times .17411$$
$$= \$8,365.$$
$$\text{Present value of future salary} = \$10,000 \times 14.591 = \$145,910.$$

The total present value of future benefits is $236,767. The total present value of future salaries is $983,750. The total of the salaries is $105,000.

Average temporary annuity = Present value of future salaries/total
                               salaries
                             = $983,750 / 105,000
                             = 9.3690476.

Normal cost = (Present value of future benefits
                − (Trust assets − credit balance))
                / Average temporary annuity
              = ($236,767 − (33,000 − 182))
              / 9.3690476
              = $21,768.

As was shown, the calculations under the aggregate funding method are simple, even in years subsequent to the initial plan year. Note, however, that the contribution levels under this method for our example are lower than under the funding methods in the previous chapters. This is because of the averaging effect of the widely differing ages of the participants.

Following are study problems regarding the aggregate funding method.

STUDY PROBLEMS

1. If the plan's projected benefit was not related to compensation, how would you calculate the average temporary annuity?

2. Why are the assets subtracted from the present value of benefits in the second and subsequent years?

3. Redo the normal cost calculation for the first plan year adding Participant 4 using the following data:

Participant 4

Age at plan inception: 42.
Age at employment: 40.
Compensation: $28,000.

CHAPTER 7

FROZEN INITIAL LIABILITY
FUNDING METHOD

The frozen initial liability funding method is a projected benefit, spread gain, aggregate-basis funding method with a past service liability. Therefore, the main difference between this funding method and the aggregate funding method, discussed in Chapter 6, is the use of a past service liability. Also, if there are plan amendments and changes in actuarial assumptions, other liability amounts would be calculated and amortized. The frozen initial liability funding method is more likely to be used for larger plans.

The frozen initial liability funding method is used because it allows flexibility in making contributions and is simple like the aggregate funding method. An employer can choose the amount of the contribution to be made as long as it falls within the calculated allowable range. Therefore, an employer can make the minimum required contribution in a lean year or the maximum deductible contribution in a good year. This flexibility makes the frozen initial liability similar to the entry age normal funding method.

Small plan sponsors have to be careful when using the frozen initial liability funding method because of the flexibility of a range of allowable contributions. Also, as under the aggregate funding method, if the participant ages are skewed, the effects of averaging can cause underfunding in small plans.

The frozen initial liability funding method calculations are illustrated using the following data.

PLAN AND INDIVIDUAL DATA USED
IN ILLUSTRATIONS

Plan Information

Normal retirement benefit: 50 percent of final year compensation.

Normal retirement age: 65.

Accrual method: current/total possible service.

Assumed interest rate: 6 percent.

Postretirement mortality: UP84 Unisex.

Contribution made on first day of first plan year: $14,000.

Trust fund balance as of first day of second plan year: $16,000.

Contribution made on last day of second plan year: $22,000.

Trust fund balance as of first day of third plan year: $40,000.

Employee Information

Participant 1

Age at plan inception: 55.

Age at employment: 40.

Compensation plan year 1: $40,000.

Compensation plan year 2: $60,000.

Compensation plan year 3: $70,000.

Participant 2

Age at plan inception: 30.

Age at employment: 25.

Compensation plan year 1: $15,000.

Compensation plan year 2: $20,000.

Compensation plan year 3: $25,000.

Participant 3

Age at employment and plan participation: 35.

Compensation plan year 3: $10,000.

Other information used in the calculations includes the annuity purchase rate derived from the interest and mortality assumptions and the applicable present value and annuity-certain factors obtained from the appendixes.

CALCULATIONS—THE FIRST PLAN YEAR

Since the frozen initial liability funding method is a projected benefit funding method, we will calculate the projected benefit for each participant as we did in previous chapters. As in the previous chapters:

Participant 1

Monthly benefit = $40,000 × 0.50 / 12 = $1,667.

Participant 2

Monthly benefit = $15,000 × 0.50 / 12 = $625.

The next step in the first year calculations is determining the past service liability. This past service liability is the same as the past service liability under the entry age normal funding method. Starting with the normal cost calculated in Chapter 4, and accumulating for the number of years between date of employment and date of plan inception, the past service liability is as follows: (Please refer to Chapter 4 for explanation of these calculations. Remember that the entry age normal cost is the cash at retirement divided by the accumulation factor of one dollar per year for the number of years from date of hire to date of retirement.)

Participant 1: $3,302 × 24.673 = $81,470.

The accumulation factor is for 15 years of past service.

Participant 2: $439 × 5.975 = $2,623.

The accumulation factor is for five years of past service.

Total = $84,093.

The past service liability is then amortized over 10 to 30 years. The normal cost calculations are done as under the aggregate funding method, except that the unfunded past service liability is subtracted from the present value of benefits.

As under the aggregate funding method, we first calculate the present value of future benefits and the present value of future salary for each participant and total these amounts. These amounts are components used to calculate the normal cost on an aggregate basis.

Present Value of Future Benefits

Participant 1: $1,667 × 115.21 × 0.55839 = $107,242.
Participant 2: $625 × 115.21 × 0.13011 = $9,369.
Total: $116,611.

Present Value of Future Salaries

Participant 1: $40,000 × 7.802 = $312,080.
Participant 2: $15,000 × 15.368 = $230,520.
Total: $542,600.

The average temporary annuity factor, as under the aggregate funding method, is the present value of future salaries divided by the total compensation.

$542,600 / 55,000 = 9.8655.

The normal cost is: (Present value of benefits − Unfunded past service liability − Assets) / Average temporary annuity factor.

($116,611 − 84,093 − 0) / 9.8655 = $3,296.

The past service liability is then amortized and the amortization amounts are added to the normal cost to determine the minimum and maximum contributions.

10-year amortization = $84,093 / 7.802 = $10,778.
30-year amortization = $84,093 / 14.591 = $5,763.
The maximum contribution = $10,778 + 3,296 = $14,074.
The minimum contribution = $5,763 + 3,296 = $9,059.

CALCULATIONS—THE SECOND PLAN YEAR

The second plan year calculations are done exactly like the first. However, the unfunded past service liability must be calculated. This amount is calculated as follows: ((Prior unfunded past service liability + Normal cost) × Interest) − (Contributions × Interest) = Unfunded past service liability.

(($84,093 + 3,296) × 1.06) − (14,000 × 1.06) = $77,792.

The second year benefit calculations are again:

Participant 1

Monthly benefit = $60,000 × 0.50 / 12 = $2,500.

Participant 2

Monthly benefit = $20,000 × 0.50 / 12 = $833.

Present Value of Future Benefits

Participant 1: $2,500 × 115.21 × 0.5919 = $170,482.
Participant 2: $833 × 115.21 × .13791 = $13,235.
Total: $183,717.

Present Value of Future Salaries

Participant 1: $60,000 × 7.21 = $432,600.
Participant 2: $20,000 × 15.230 = $304,600.
Total: $737,200.

Average Temporary Annuity

$737,200 / $80,000 = 9.215.

Normal Cost

Normal cost = (Present value of future benefits − Unfunded liability
           − Assets) / Average temporary annuity
         = (183,717 − 77,792 − 16,000) / 9.215
         = $9,759.

The maximum contribution is $10,778 + 9,759 = $20,537. The minimum contribution is $5,763 + 9,759 = $15,522.

CALCULATIONS—THE THIRD PLAN YEAR

The third year calculations are complicated by the addition of a new employee. As in the second year, we first calculate the unfunded past service liability under the following formula: ((Prior unfunded past service liability + Normal cost) × Interest) − (Contributions × Interest) = Unfunded past service liability. Note that since the contribution was made on the last day of the year, we do not add interest. Unfunded past service liability = (($77,792 + 9,759) × 1.06) − 22,000 = $70,804. No interest is added to the contribution, because it was made at the end of the year.

As before, we now calculate the monthly benefits, present value of future benefits, and present value of future salaries for each participant.

Participant 1

$$\text{Monthly benefit} = \$70,000 \times 0.50 / 12$$
$$= \$2,917.$$
$$\text{Present value of future benefits} = \$2,917 \times 115.21 \times .62741$$
$$= \$210,852.$$
$$\text{Present value of future salaries} = \$70,000 \times 6.582$$
$$= \$460,740.$$

Participant 2

$$\text{Monthly benefit} = \$25,000 \times 0.50 / 12$$
$$= \$1,042.$$
$$\text{Present value of future benefits} = \$1,042 \times 115.21 \times .14619$$
$$= \$17,550.$$
$$\text{Present value of future salaries} = \$25,000 \times 15.084$$
$$= \$377,100.$$

Participant 3

$$\text{Monthly benefit} = \$10,000 \times 0.50 / 12$$
$$= \$417.$$
$$\text{Present value of future benefits} = \$417 \times 115.21 \times .17411$$
$$= \$8,365.$$
$$\text{Present value of future salaries} = \$10,000 \times 14.591$$
$$= \$145,910.$$

The total present value of future benefits = $236,767. The total present value of future salaries = $983,750. The total salaries = $105,000.

Average temporary annuity = Present value of future salaries / Salaries
= \$983,750 / 105,000
= 9.3690476.

Normal cost = (Present value of future benefits
— Unfunded past service liability
— Assets) / Average temporary
annuity
= (\$236,767 — 70,804
— 40,000) / 9.3690476
= \$13,445.

The maximum contribution is \$13,445 + 10,778 = \$24,223. The minimum contribution is \$13,445 + 5,763 = \$19,208.

STUDY PROBLEMS

1. When the past service liability is fully amortized, what is the effect on the frozen initial liability funding method?

2. Calculate the normal cost under the frozen initial liability funding method (for the first plan year) adding the following participant:

Participant 4:

Age at plan participation: 44.
Age at employment: 45.
Compensation: \$32,000.

PART 3

ACCRUED BENEFIT FUNDING METHODS

CHAPTER 8

UNIT CREDIT FUNDING
METHOD

The unit credit funding method is an accrued benefit, immediate gain, individual-basis funding method with a past service liability. This funding method is significantly different from those previously covered. It is based on the benefit accrued to date, rather than the projected benefit.

The unit credit funding method is used mainly when the benefit is a flat dollar amount times years of service. Since it has a past service liability to amortize, it traditionally allowed flexibility in making contributions similar to the entry age normal and frozen initial liability funding methods.

When a plan's benefit formula is related to compensation, a variation of unit credit funding method should be used. It is known as the projected unit credit funding method. The projected unit credit funding method is discussed in Chapter 9. Since this chapter covers the traditional unit credit funding method, we use a different normal retirement benefit (not dependent on compensation) in the examples.

As in the entry age normal and frozen initial liability funding methods, small plan sponsors have to be careful when using the unit credit funding method, again because of the flexibility of a range of allowable contributions and the danger of underfunding. However, small plans rarely have a flat-dollar type of retirement benefit and, therefore, would be unlikely to use the traditional unit credit funding method.

The unit credit funding method calculations are illustrated using the following data.

PLAN AND INDIVIDUAL DATA USED
IN ILLUSTRATIONS

Plan Information

Normal retirement benefit: $60 per month times years of service.
Normal retirement age: 65.
Accrual method: benefit accrued by formula.
Assumed interest rate: 6 percent.
Postretirement mortality: UP84 Unisex.
Contribution made on first day of first plan year: $12,000.
Trust fund balance as of first day of second plan year: $13,000.
Contribution made on last day of second plan year: $10,000.
Trust fund balance as of first day of third plan year: $25,000.

Employee Information

Participant 1

Age at plan inception: 55.
Age at employment: 40.
Compensation plan year 1: $40,000.
Compensation plan year 2: $60,000.
Compensation plan year 3: $70,000.

Participant 2

Age at plan inception: 30.
Age at employment: 25.
Compensation plan year 1: $15,000.
Compensation plan year 2: $20,000.
Compensation plan year 3: $25,000.

Participant 3

Age at employment and plan participation: 35.
Compensation plan year 3: $10,000.

Other information to be used in the calculations includes the annuity purchase rate derived from the interest and mortality assumptions and the applicable present value and annuity-certain factors obtained from the appendixes.

CALCULATIONS—THE FIRST PLAN YEAR

Since the unit credit funding method is based on the accrued benefit, we first calculate the accrued benefit for each participant. Recall that the accrued benefit is the portion of the normal retirement benefit that has accrued to the participant as a result of service performed to date. It is usually a monthly amount that the participant will begin to receive at normal retirement age. Using the above normal retirement benefit and accrual method, the calculations are as follows:

Participant 1

$$\$60 \times 15 \text{ years} = \$900.$$

(Participant 1 worked for the company 15 years at the time of plan inception.)

Participant 2

$$\$60 \times 5 \text{ years} = \$300.$$

(Participant 2 worked for the company five years at the time of plan inception.)

The past service liability under the accrued benefit funding method is the present value of these accrued benefits. The past service liability is determined as follows:

Participant 1: $\$900 \times 115.21 \times 0.55839 = \$57,899.$
Participant 2: $\$300 \times 115.21 \times .13011 = \$4,497.$
Total: $\$62,396.$

The past service liability is amortized over 10 to 30 years. Ten-year amortization would be: $\$62,396 / 7.802 = \$7,997.$ Thirty-year amortization would be: $\$62,396 / 14.591 = \$4,276.$

The normal cost is calculated next. Under the unit credit funding method, the normal cost is simply the present value of the benefit accruing during the year. The calculations follow:

Participant 1

$$\$60 \times 115.21 \times 0.55839 = \$3,860.$$

Participant 2

$$\$60 \times 115.21 \times 0.13011 = \$899.$$

Therefore, the total normal cost is $\$3,860 + 899 = \$4,759$. The present value of one dollar factor was for 10 years for Participant 1 and 35 years for Participant 2.

Adding the normal cost to the amortization payment, the maximum contribution would be $\$7,997 + 4,759 = \$12,756$. The minimum contribution would be $\$4,276 + 4,759 = \$9,035$.

CALCULATIONS—THE SECOND PLAN YEAR

The second year calculations are complicated by the actuarial gain or loss determination. The actuarial gain or loss is calculated in the same manner as under the entry age normal or individual level premium funding methods. It is the difference between the expected unfunded liability and the actual unfunded liability. First, let us determine the second year normal cost.

Participant 1

$$\$60 \times 115.21 \times 0.5919 = \$4,092.$$

Participant 2

$$\$60 \times 115.21 \times 0.13791 = \$953.$$

The total normal cost is $\$4,092 + 953 = \$5,045$. Note that the present value of one dollar factors were for 9 years for Participant 1 and 34 years for Participant 2.

The accrued liability is the present value of the benefit accrued so far and is calculated individually for each participant and then added. The calculations follow:

Participant 1: $\$60 \times 16$ years $\times 115.21 \times 0.5919 = \$65,465$.
Participant 2: $\$60 \times 6$ years $\times 115.21 \times 0.13791 = \$5,720.00$.
Total accrued liability $= \$71,185$.

The unfunded liability is the accrued liability minus the trust assets = $71,185 − 13,000 = $58,185.

The expected unfunded liability is calculated as follows:

Prior unfunded liability	$62,396
+ Prior normal cost	+4,759
=	$67,155
× 1.06	$71,184
− Contribution × interest	− 12,720
=	$58,464.

Therefore, the actuarial gain is the expected unfunded liability minus the actual unfunded liability = $58,464 − 58,185 = $279. This amount amortized over five years is $62. This amount amortized over 10 years is $36. The maximum contribution is $5,045 + 7,997 − 36 = $13,006. The minimum contribution is $5,045 + 4,276 − 62 = $9,259. As shown, an actuarial gain is subtracted from the normal cost; an actuarial loss would have been added.

CALCULATIONS—THE THIRD PLAN YEAR

The third year calculations are complicated by the addition of a new participant. Otherwise, we follow the same steps as in the second year calculations. First, let's determine the third year normal cost and then the actuarial gain or loss.

Normal Cost

Participant 1: $60 × 115.21 × .62741 = $4,337.
Participant 2: $60 × 115.21 × .14619 = $1,011.
Participant 3: $60 × 115.21 × .17411 = $1,204.
Total normal cost = $6,552.

Actuarial Gain or Loss

To calculate the actuarial gain or loss, we need to calculate the components. Remember that the gain or loss is the expected unfunded liability minus the actual unfunded liability. The unfunded liability is the accrued liability minus the trust assets. The accrued liability is the present value of the accrued benefit.

Accrued Liability

Participant 1: $60 \times 17 \times 115.21 \times .62741 = \$73,730.$
Participant 2: $60 \times 7 \times 115.21 \times .14619 = \$7,074.$
Participant 3: No accrued benefit to date, as was just hired.
Total accrued liability = $80,804.
Unfunded liability = $80,804 − 25,000 = $55,804.

Expected Unfunded Liability

Prior unfunded liability	$58,185
+ Prior normal cost	5,045
=	63,230
63,230 × 1.06	67,024
− Contribution	10,000
=	$57,024.

No interest was added to the contribution because it was made on the last day of the plan year.

The actuarial gain or loss = $57,024 − 55,804 = $1,220. The amortization of this gain over five years is $1,220 / 4.465 = $273. The amortization of this gain over 10 years is $1,220 / 7.802 = $156.

With the amortization of this gain to the normal cost, amortization of the past service liability, and amortization of the previous gain, the maximum contribution = $6,552 + 7,997 − 36 − 156 = $14,357. The minimum contribution = $6,552 + 4,276 − 62 − 273 = $10,493.

STUDY PROBLEMS

1. How are the first year and second year normal costs related? Why?

2. Under the other funding methods, our second year examples showed much higher contributions in the second year. Why is this not true under this chapter's example?

3. Why were the $62 and $273 amortization amounts subtracted rather than added to the normal cost and past service liability amortization amounts?

CHAPTER 9

VARIATIONS AND COMBINATION FUNDING METHODS

This chapter reviews combination funding methods and insured small plans. Combination funding methods combine parts of various funding methods already discussed. Since the concepts and calculations were discussed in previous chapters, full calculations are not done in this chapter.

PROJECTED UNIT CREDIT FUNDING METHOD

The projected unit credit funding method is nearly identical to the traditional unit credit funding method discussed in Chapter 8. There is one important difference, however, that facilitates use with salary-related benefit formulas. Under the projected unit credit funding method, the projected normal retirement benefit is calculated. Then the accrued benefit is calculated based on the projected normal retirement benefit. In most cases, the projected normal retirement benefit is calculated using a salary scale. This means the actuary assumes that pay raises occur during plan participation. (See Chapter 10 for discussion of salary scales.) The remaining calculations are done under the traditional unit credit funding method. An example follows:

Suppose the participant has five years to work until normal retirement age. The actuary assumes he will receive a pay raise of 3 percent each year. The normal retirement benefit is 50 percent of final salary, and his current salary is $20,000.

Step 1: We determine the final salary using the pay raise assumption. Using the accumulation of one dollar, $20,000 × 1.159 = $23,180.

Step 2: Determine the projected monthly normal retirement benefit: $23,180 × 0.50 / 12 = $966.

Step 3: We determine the accrued benefit (for the past service liability or accrued liability) and the benefit accruing during the year (for the normal cost). We use the projected normal retirement benefit with the salary scale for these calculations. For our example, assume the accrued benefit is based on the number of years of service divided by total possible years of service, and our participant has five years of prior service. His accrued benefit fraction is 5/10. Therefore, his accrued benefit for purposes of these calculations is $966 × .5 = $483. The benefit accruing during the year is $966 × 1/10 = $97. (Note, however, that prorating over service is not always permissible under the projected unit credit method under Internal Revenue Code Reg. 1.412(c)(3)-1.)

Step 4: The remaining calculations are done under the traditional unit credit funding method, using the amounts determined in Step 3. These calculations should be done for Study Problem 1.

As mentioned previously, this funding method is used rather than the traditional unit credit funding method when the normal retirement benefit is salary-related. If the traditional unit credit funding method were used with a salary-related formula, the plan costs would become unreasonable as salary increases were given, and the plan would run the risk of being underfunded. The projected unit credit funding method is developed to allow the costs to be spread more evenly over the years of participation.

The projected unit credit funding method is becoming important for another reason. The Financial Accounting Standards Board requires use of this funding method for determining pension liability to be reported on audited financial statements. While this rule will affect large companies more often than small companies, use of this funding method will probably increase for all size plans. The Financial Accounting Standards Board Statement 87 details the pension reporting for financial statement purposes.

ATTAINED AGE NORMAL FUNDING METHOD

The attained age normal funding method combines aspects of the unit credit funding method and the frozen initial liability funding method. As you will recall, the past service liability under the frozen initial liability funding method is determined as if the entry age normal funding method were used. Then calculations similar to those under the frozen initial liability funding method are done. The only difference between the frozen initial liability funding method and the attained age normal funding method is that the past service liability is determined under the unit credit funding method, not the entry age normal funding method. For Study Problem 2, use the participant and plan data in Chapter 7 and recalculate the first year normal cost and past service liability using the attained age normal funding method.

INSURED PLANS

Traditionally, many small plans have life insurance policies to cover plan death benefits. Usually, whole-life or universal-life policies are used because these types of insurance have cash values. Some very small plans are fully insured, which means the cash value at retirement is enough to pay retirement benefits. However, most insured plans also have a trust fund.

There are two methods for considering the cash values when determining plan costs. These methods can be used under any funding method, but the individual-type funding methods are usually used because the policies are normally written for each participant. Additional policies are usually written as benefits are increased. In fact, the individual level premium funding method is ideal for insured plans because benefit increases requiring new policies are tracked on a year-by-year basis.

Split-Funded Method

The split-funded method of considering cash values is used when the insurance is whole life. With whole-life insurance, the cash value at retirement is fixed and is known when the policy is purchased. Therefore, the actuary knows how much cash at retirement will be available from the life insurance policies and how much cash at retirement must be available in the trust fund. Therefore, the normal costs need cover only the necessary cash at retirement, excluding the policies' cash value at retirement. An example follows:

Using the plan and participant information in Chapter 3, assume a whole-life policy is purchased for Participant 1. The policy has a cash value at age 65 of $50,000. Therefore, before the normal cost is calculated, we must subtract $50,000 from the total cash at retirement amount of $192,055. Therefore, the first year normal cost would be:

$$(192{,}055 - 50{,}000) / 13.972 = \$10{,}167.$$

Then the annual premium would be added to the normal cost to determine the total cost for the plan year.

Envelope Method

The envelope method of considering cash values is used with universal-life policies. Generally, universal-life policies are interest-sensitive, and the cash values vary with investment earnings. Therefore, the cash value at normal retirement age is not known. The cash value for the year is known, however. This cash value is added to the trust asset amount when doing the calculations. The cost of insurance is added to the normal cost to determine the total plan cost for a year. An example follows:

Suppose the cash value in the second year is $1,000, and we are using the data in Chapter 3. Under the envelope method of considering cash values, we would simply add $1,000 to $16,000 and use this amount as the asset value. For Study Problem 3, recalculate the actuarial gain or loss, using $17,000 as the market value of assets.

PART 4

INTRODUCTION TO ADVANCED ACTUARIAL TOPICS

CHAPTER 10

ACTUARIAL ASSUMPTIONS: EFFECTS ON FUNDING

OVERVIEW

In Chapters 3 through 9, the simplest actuarial assumptions were used, emphasizing the funding method concepts and calculations. The computation process was not confused by complicated actuarial assumptions. In fact, most small plans actually do use only the simplest assumptions.

What Is an Actuarial Assumption?

An actuarial assumption is something the plan's actuary can reasonably expect to occur in plan experience. The actuary assumes the event will occur for purposes of the calculations. For example, an actuary can assume some participants will die, terminate employment, become disabled, and retire. Some participants retire early, some late, and some retire on their normal retirement date. In addition, the actuary assumes the trust fund set up for the plan will have earnings on its investments. The actuary can assume employees will receive pay raises. Plan administrative expenses can be assumed. Assumptions may vary by employee type, age, and number of years of service. The assumptions can be based on prior plan experience, the actuary's experience with similar plans, or various standard tables.

What Assumptions Are Normally Used for Small Plans?

Generally, the actuary for a small plan uses an investment earnings assumption, a postretirement mortality assumption, and perhaps a salary scale. In Chapters 3 through 8, investment earning and postretirement mortality assumptions were used. In Chapter 9, a salary scale was used to illustrate the projected unit credit funding method. An actuary for a small plan usually assumes a participant will retire on his or her normal retirement date. In our examples, the normal retirement date was assumed for all participants.

Assumptions such as preretirement mortality, disability, and turnover are rarely used by actuaries for small plans. While participants in small plans do die, become disabled, or quit, there is not a pattern to these occurrences. For example, a preretirement mortality table may specify that 0.09 percent of participants age 30 will die. Obviously, if there are only 10 participants and one of them is age 30, this assumption doesn't make sense. Most small plans have some sort of death and disability benefit, so the plan does not normally have a large actuarial gain if someone dies or becomes disabled. In addition, most plans usually have fast vesting, so there is only a small actuarial gain due to participant's termination of service. (Vesting is briefly discussed in the section on turnover assumptions.)

The following sections include descriptions of and the effects of the most commonly used assumptions.

INVESTMENT EARNINGS

When calculating plan costs, actuaries always consider growth of the plan's trust fund. ERISA requires prudent investment by trustees, so the trust fund should always have long-term investment objectives. Of course, earnings vary depending on the market, safety of investments, amount of investments, and perhaps luck. Therefore, the actuary changes the investment earnings (interest) assumption from time to time.

Many actuaries for small plans adjust their interest assumption to compensate for not using a variety of more complex actuarial assumptions. The assumptions are known as implicit assumptions rather than explicit assumptions. As long as the adjustment is reasonable, use of implicit assumptions is usually fine for calculations of contributions. However, the Financial Accounting Standards Board Statement 87 requires the use of explicit assumptions for most financial statement pension cost calculations. In addition, the Pension Protection Act of 1987 adds the following requirement relating the actuarial assumptions:

In the case of . . . (i) a plan other than a multiemployer plan, each of which is reasonable (taking into account the experience of the plan and reasonable expectations) of which, in the aggregate, result in a total contribution equivalent to that which would be determined if each such assumption and method were reasonable. . . .

The Pension Protection Act of 1987 gives guidelines to follow when choosing an interest rate assumption for calculating current liability (Chapter 13). The interest rate cannot be more than 10 percent above or below the weighted average of the rates of interest on 30-year Treasury securities during the 4-year period ending on the last day before the beginning of the plan year.

Use of an interest assumption lowers the contribution because it is assumed some of the cash to pay benefits will come from investment earnings. Figure 10–1 illustrates the difference in first year normal cost

FIGURE 10–1
First Year Normal Cost for Participant 1 with Various Interest Rate Assumptions

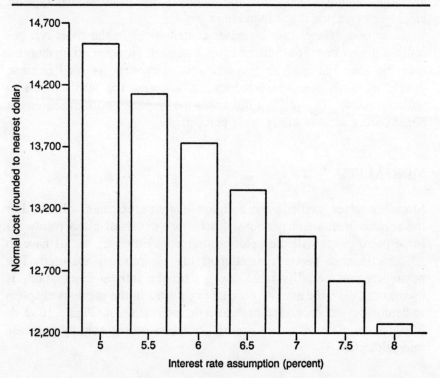

using various interest rates. (Interest rates chosen for use in this book are for illustration purposes and cannot be relied on in all cases to be "reasonable" and satisfying the Pension Protection Act of 1987.)

SALARY SCALE

When a plan's benefit formula is related to compensation, use of a salary scale helps keep plan costs from skyrocketing as pay increases occur. By predicting pay increases, the actuary can keep a more level contribution over the years. The mathematics of salary scales is discussed in Chapter 9 under the projected unit credit funding method section. Salaries can be assumed to increase each year by a certain percentage for all participants. Or salary projections can depend on the age and type of employee.

Some small plans do not have a salary scale assumption because participants are already at the maximum benefit under Internal Revenue Code Section 415 (discussed in Chapter 12). Others do not have a salary scale assumption because the nature of the business and type of employees preclude much increase in pay.

Use of a salary scale increases contributions in the short run because a higher benefit at retirement is assumed. However, contributions over the long run may be less when a salary scale is used because benefit increases are considered earlier, allowing the plan's assets to build up sooner. Figure 10–2 illustrates the projected normal retirement benefit using various salary scale percentages.

MORTALITY

Mortality tables predict when and how many participants will die. For the reasons mentioned previously, actuaries for small plans rarely assume participants will die before retirement. However, we all have to go sometime, so postretirement mortality assumptions are used. The postretirement mortality table, along with the interest assumption, is used to calculate the annuity purchase rate used in the previous chapters to determine the necessary cash at retirement amount. Figure 10–3 illustrates the effect of various mortality tables on the annuity purchase rate calculation.

FIGURE 10–2
First Year Projected Normal Retirement Benefit* for Participant 1 with Various Salary Scales

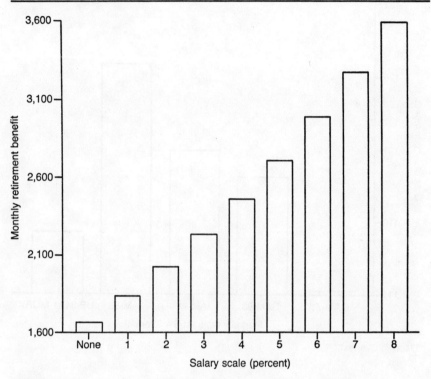

*Benefit projected using compensation first plan year, with 10 years until normal retirement.

Use of a mortality assumption reduces plan contributions because benefits are generally assumed to stop when a participant dies.

TURNOVER

When an actuary assumes a number of participants will terminate employment before receiving benefits, he or she is using a turnover assumption. Generally, small plans do not use turnover assumptions because the group size is too small. Also, small businesses are likely to replace terminated employees immediately at approximately the same rate of pay.

FIGURE 10–3
Mortality Tables—Effects on Annuity Purchase Rate at 65

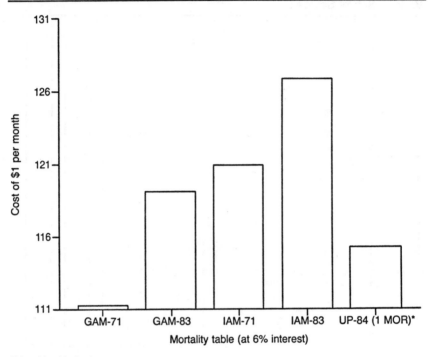

*Used in this text.

Turnover assumptions reduce plan contributions because fewer participants are expected to receive benefits. Vesting schedules can offset the effect of the turnover assumption. Vesting is making portions of a participant's accrued benefit nonforfeitable. This means that even participants who quit before retirement will receive some retirement benefit, if they are vested.

Many sophisticated assumptions can be developed and used by actuaries in determining plan costs. A thorough discussion of all assumptions is beyond the scope of an introductory text.

CHAPTER 11

MINIMUM FUNDING STANDARD ACCOUNT

OVERVIEW

Once the defined benefit plan calculations have been done under one of the funding methods described in Chapters 3 through 9, the numbers are used by the employer in several ways. A company's auditors must show a pension expense on the financial statements. A company's tax consultant needs to ascertain whether a plan contribution is a deductible expense. The actuary normally assists these professionals and the employer in determining the proper amounts for those purposes. However, the actuary's main concern is determining whether the plan is properly funded. That is, the actuary must calculate the proper contributions so there will be enough money to pay benefits when due and report whether these contributions are made. This task is done under the minimum funding standard account.

The concept of minimum funding standards was first set forth in the Employee Retirement Income Security Act of 1974 (ERISA). The Internal Revenue Code's Section 412 and regulations thereunder explain use of the minimum funding standard account.

In addition to nearly all defined benefit plans, defined contribution plans such as money purchase and target plans are covered under the minimum funding standard rules. Plans that are not covered are:

Profit sharing or stock bonus plans.
Certain insurance contract plans.
Governmental plans.
Church plans not electing coverage.
Plans with no employer contributions since ERISA.

Plans established by associations under which no contributions are made by the employers of the participants.

Under a defined contribution plan, minimum funding standards are satisfied if the proper contributions, as set forth in the plan documents, are made in a timely fashion. Timely contributions must be made within 8 1/2 months after the plan year ends.

Minimum funding standard calculations are more complicated under a defined benefit plan. The calculations depend on the type of funding method used. The funding methods can be categorized in two ways. In calculating for minimum funding standard purposes, the funding methods are differentiated by whether they:

Have a separate supplemental liability or experience gain to amortize (see Chapter 2).

Have a directly calculated accrued liability (individual level premium, entry age normal, and unit credit methods).

Having a directly calculated accrued liability affects calculation of the full funding limitation, which will be discussed later in this chapter.

Supplemental liabilities (the past service cost) are amortized over 30 years for purposes of the minimum funding standard account. (The supplemental liability is amortized over 40 years for plans that began before January 1, 1974.) Actuarial experience gains or losses are amortized over five years. (For plan years beginning before 1988, actuarial gains or losses are amortized over 15 years.)

Actuaries must follow certain special rules under Internal Revenue Code Section 412 when applying minimum funding standards. These rules are:

The valuation of trust assets must take fair market value into account under 412 regulations.

Actuarial assumptions must be reasonable (see Chapter 10).

Changes in funding method or plan year requires Internal Revenue Service approval. However, approval is not necessary if the change is to an acceptable method under applicable revenue rulings.

The full funding limitation must be calculated (see later section of this chapter).

Certain retroactive plan amendments will be deemed to be in effect as of the first day of the plan year.

Actuarial valuations must be done at least once every three years.

Contributions must be made within 8 1/2 months after the plan year end to be considered as contributions for that year. For plan years beginning in 1989, however, quarterly payments must be made under 412(m) of the Internal Revenue Code.

EXAMPLES OF SIMPLE MINIMUM FUNDING STANDARD ACCOUNTS

To illustrate simple minimum funding standard accounts, the calculations done in Chapters 3, 4, and 6 will be used. The minimum funding standard account for a defined benefit plan is reported to the Internal Revenue Service on the Schedule B attachment to the Annual Return/ Report 5500. (A Schedule B must also be attached to 5500 alternatives such as the 5500-C, 5500-R, and 5500-EZ.) The minimum funding standard account section 9 of the 1987 Schedule B is used in the illustrations.

Individual Level Premium Funding Method

First, we will calculate the minimum funding standard account under the individual level premium funding method using the calculations in Chapter 3. Both the first and second plan years are shown. Let's assume the first plan year is calendar year 1988. The minimum funding standard account is shown in Figure 11–1.

A full year of interest at 6 percent is calculated on the normal cost. This is because the valuation calculations were done as of the first day of the plan year. If an end-of-year valuation were prepared, interest would not be applicable and would not be included on line 9d.

A full year's interest at 6 percent is also calculated on the contribution. This is because our data indicated the contribution was made on the first day of the plan year. Had the contribution been made on another date during the plan year, the interest would be prorated. For example, if the contribution had been made on July 17, 1988, interest would be calculated as follows:

$$\$15,200 \times 0.06 \times 167/365 = \$417.$$

FIGURE 11–1

Schedule B (Form 5500) 1987 — Page 2

8 Funding standard account and other information:

a Accrued liabilities as determined for funding standard account as of (enter date) ▶ .... ____

b Value of assets as determined for funding standard account as of (enter date) ▶ .... ____

c Unfunded liability for spread-gain methods with bases as of (enter date) ▶ .... ____

d (i) Actuarial gains or (losses) for period ending ▶ .... ____
(ii) Shortfall gains or (losses) for period ending ▶ .... ____

e Amount of contribution certified by the actuary as necessary to reduce the funding deficiency to zero, from 9m or 10h (or the attachment for 4b if required) . . . . ____

9 Funding standard account statement for this plan year ending ▶ 12/31/88

Charges to funding standard account:

a Prior year funding deficiency, if any	0
b Employer's normal cost for plan year as of mo. _1_ day _1_ yr. _88_	14356
c Amortization charges	
(i) Funding waivers (outstanding balance as of mo. ..... day ..... yr. ..... ▶ $ ....)	0
(ii) Other than waivers (outstanding balance as of mo. ..... day ..... yr. ..... ▶ $ ....)	0
d Interest as applicable to the end of the plan year on a, b, and c	861
e Total charges (add a through d)	15217

Credits to funding standard account:

f Prior year credit balance, if any	0
g Employer contributions (total from column (b) of item 7)	15200
h Amortization credits (outstanding balance as of mo. ..... day ..... yr. ..... ▶ $ ....)	0
i Interest as applicable to end of plan year on f, g, and h	912
j Other (specify) ▶	0
k Total credits (add f through j)	16112

Balance:

l Credit balance: if k is greater than e, enter the difference	895
m Funding deficiency: if e is greater than k, enter the difference	

10 Alternative minimum funding standard account (omit if not used):

a Was the entry age normal cost method used to determine entries in item 9 above? . . . . ☐ Yes ☐ No
If "No," do not complete b through h.

b Prior year alternate funding deficiency, if any . . . . ____

c Normal cost . . . . ____

d Excess, if any, of value of accrued benefits over market value of assets . . . . . . ____

e Interest on b, c, and d . . . . ____

f Employer contributions (total from column (b) of item 7) . . . . ____

g Interest on f . . . . ____

h Funding deficiency: if the sum of b through e is greater than the sum of f and g, enter difference . . ____

11 Actuarial cost method used as the basis for this plan year's funding standard account computation:

a ☐ Attained age normal   **b** ☐ Entry age normal   **c** ☐ Accrued benefit (unit credit)

d ☐ Aggregate   **e** ☐ Frozen initial liability   **f** ☐ Individual level premium

g ☐ Other (specify) ▶

12 Checklist of certain actuarial assumptions:

	A Used for item 6d and e—value of accrued benefits				B Used for item 8, 9 or 10—funding standard account			
	Pre-retirement		Post-retirement		Pre-retirement		Post-retirement	
	Yes	No	Yes	No	Yes	No	Yes	No
a Rates specified in insurance or annuity contracts								
b Mortality table code:								
(i) Males								
(ii) Females								
c Interest rate		%		%		%		%
d Retirement age								
e Expense loading		%		%		%		%

	Male	Female		Male	Female	
f Annual withdrawal rate:						
(i) Age 25	%	%		%	%	
(ii) Age 40	%	%		%	%	
(iii) Age 55	%	%		%	%	
g Ratio of salary at normal retirement to salary at:						
(i) Age 25				%	%	
(ii) Age 40				%	%	
(iii) Age 55				%	%	

h Is a statement of actuarial assumptions, actuarial funding method, etc., attached? . . . . . . ☐ Yes ☐ No

For the second year's minimum funding standard account under the individual level premium funding method, let's assume a contribution of $22,800 was made on September 30, 1989. The account would be as shown in Figure 11–2.

Because there was an actuarial loss, there was an additional charge in the funding standard account. If there had been a gain, there would be an additional credit. According to Section 412 of the Internal Revenue Code, actuarial gains and losses must be amortized over five years for purposes of minimum funding. Each gain or loss must be tracked for five years. The outstanding balance of each gain or loss decreases each year until fully amortized. However, all gains are aggregated and all losses are aggregated for purposes of Part 9 of the Schedule B. An example of the calculation of the third year outstanding balance of the second year's loss follows. It is the last outstanding balance minus the amortization payment times interest.

$$(\$895 - 200) \times 1.06 = \$737.$$

(If, for example, there is a loss in the third year of $4,000, the total outstanding balance would be $4,737, and the amortization payment would be $200 + 896 = $1,096.)

The interest on line 9d includes interest on both the normal cost and the amortization payment.

On the credit portion, the credit balance from the prior year is brought forward. A full year's interest is added to the credit balance on line 9i.

The fact that the credit balance is brought forward each year with interest can be of great significance to the plan sponsor. Each year that the employer contributes more than is necessary to satisfy minimum funding requirements builds a reserve for future years. If for a certain year, the credit balance grew to $25,000, and the total charges on line 9e were only $23,000, the employer would not need to make any contribution. This could be a lifesaver when an employer is enduring hard times.

Line 9i includes interest on the contribution as well as interest on the credit balance. The interest on the contribution is calculated as follows:

$$\$22,800 \times 0.06 \times 92/365 = \$345.$$

FIGURE 11–2

Schedule B (Form 5500) 1987		Page **2**

8 Funding standard account and other information:

a Accrued liabilities as determined for funding standard account as of (enter date) ▶ ....

b Value of assets as determined for funding standard account as of (enter date) ▶ ....

c Unfunded liability for spread-gain methods with bases as of (enter date) ▶ ....

d (i) Actuarial gains or (losses) for period ending ▶ ....

   (ii) Shortfall gains or (losses) for period ending ▶ ....

e Amount of contribution certified by the actuary as necessary to reduce the funding deficiency to zero, from 9m or 10h (or the attachment for 4b if required) ....

9 Funding standard account statement for this plan year ending ▶ .... 12/31/89 ....

Charges to funding standard account:

a Prior year funding deficiency, if any	0
b Employer's normal cost for plan year as of mo. 1 day 1 yr. 89	22452
c Amortization charges	
(i) Funding waivers (outstanding balance is of mo. 1 day 1 yr. 89 ▶ $ ....)	0
(ii) Other than waivers (outstanding balance as of mo. .... day .... yr. .... ▶ $ 895)	200
d Interest as applicable to the end of the plan year on a, b, and c	1359
e Total charges (add a through d)	24011

Credits to funding standard account:

f Prior year credit balance, if any	895
g Employer contributions (total from column (b) of item 7)	22800
h Amortization credits (outstanding balance as of mo. .... day .... yr. .... ▶ $ ....)	0
i Interest as applicable to end of plan year on f, g, and h	399
j Other (specify) ▶	0
k Total credits (add f through j)	24094

Balance:

l Credit balance: if k is greater than e, enter the difference	83
m Funding deficiency: if e is greater than k, enter the difference	0

10 Alternative minimum funding standard account (omit if not used):

a Was the entry age normal cost method used to determine entries in item 9 above? ☐ Yes ☐ No

If "No," do not complete b through h.

b Prior year alternate funding deficiency, if any

c Normal cost

d Excess, if any, of value of accrued benefits over market value of assets

e Interest on b, c, and d

f Employer contributions (total from column (b) of item 7)

g Interest on f

h Funding deficiency: if the sum of b through e is greater than the sum of f and g, enter difference

11 Actuarial cost method used as the basis for this plan year's funding standard account computation:

a ☐ Attained age normal   **b** ☐ Entry age normal   **c** ☐ Accrued benefit (unit credit)

d ☐ Aggregate   **e** ☐ Frozen initial liability   **f** ☐ Individual level premium

g ☐ Other (specify) ▶

12 Checklist of certain actuarial assumptions:

	A Used for item 6d and e—value of accrued benefits				B Used for item 8, 9 or 10—funding standard account			
	Pre-retirement		Post-retirement		Pre-retirement		Post-retirement	
	Yes	No	Yes	No	Yes	No	Yes	No
a Rates specified in insurance or annuity contracts								
b Mortality table code:								
(i) Males								
(ii) Females								
c Interest rate		%		%		%		%
d Retirement age								
e Expense loading		%		%		%		%

	Male	Female		Male	Female	
f Annual withdrawal rate:						
(i) Age 25	%	%		%	%	
(ii) Age 40	%	%		%	%	
(iii) Age 55	%	%		%	%	
g Ratio of salary at normal retirement to salary at:						
(i) Age 25				%	%	
(ii) Age 40				%	%	
(iii) Age 55				%	%	

h Is a statement of actuarial assumptions, actuarial funding method, etc., attached? ☐ Yes ☐ No

Entry Age Normal Funding Method

Next we will determine the first and second year minimum funding standard account under the entry age normal funding method, using the calculations from Chapter 4. The funding standard account is similar to the individual level premium minimum funding standard account except there are amortization charges in the first year and the outstanding balance of the first year amortization base must be calculated for the second year. This outstanding balance is calculated as follows:

$$(\$84{,}093 - 5{,}763) \times 1.06 = \$83{,}030.$$

The second year's amortization amounts (both outstanding balance and payment) include the actuarial experience loss from the second year.

The first and second year's minimum funding standard accounts are as shown in Figures 11–3 and 11–4.

The credit balance under the entry age normal funding method can become quite large, and the credit balance can grow much quicker than it could under the individual level premium funding method. The large difference between the minimum required contribution and the maximum deductible contribution makes the growth possible. If the employer makes the maximum deductible contribution for several years, the credit balance grows quickly. As discussed in Chapter 4, many actuaries choose this funding method to allow plan sponsors more flexibility in making contributions. As mentioned under the previous section, this flexibility can be a great help when the employer has an unprofitable year.

Aggregate Funding Method

The following shows the minimum funding standard account for the first and second years under the aggregate funding method. Since the aggregate funding method does not have separately calculated actuarial gains or supplement past service liability amounts, the account is straightforward. For the second year's account, let's assume a contribution of $19,640 is made on December 31, 1989. The funding standard accounts would be as in Figures 11–5 and 11–6.

FIGURE 11–3

Schedule B (Form 5500) 1987 — Page 2

8 Funding standard account and other information:
- **a** Accrued liabilities as determined for funding standard account as of (enter date) ▶ ....
- **b** Value of assets as determined for funding standard account as of (enter date) ▶ ....
- **c** Unfunded liability for spread-gain methods with bases as of (enter date) ▶ ....
- **d** *(i)* Actuarial gains or (losses) for period ending ▶ ....
  (ii) Shortfall gains or (losses) for period ending ▶ ....
- **e** Amount of contribution certified by the actuary as necessary to reduce the funding deficiency to zero, from 9m or 10h (or the attachment for 4b if required) . . . .

9 Funding standard account statement for this plan year ending ▶ 12/31/88

Charges to funding standard account:
- **a** Prior year funding deficiency, if any . . . . — 0
- **b** Employer's normal cost for plan year as of mo. 1 day 1 yr. 88 . . . . . . — 3741
- **c** Amortization charges
  (i) Funding waivers (outstanding balance as of mo. ..... day ..... yr. ..... ▶ $ ....)
  (ii) Other than waivers (outstanding balance as of mo. 1 day 1 yr. 88 ▶ $ 84093 ..) — 5763
- **d** Interest as applicable to the end of the plan year on a, b, and c . . . . — 570
- **e** Total charges (add a through d) . . . . — 10074

Credits to funding standard account:
- **f** Prior year credit balance, if any . . . . — 0
- **g** Employer contributions (total from column (b) of item 7) . . . . — 15200
- **h** Amortization credits (outstanding balance as of mo. ..... day ..... yr. ..... ▶ $ ....) — 0
- **i** Interest as applicable to end of plan year on f, g, and h . . . . — 912
- **j** Other (specify) ▶ .... — 0
- **k** Total credits (add f through j) . . . . — 16112

Balance:
- **l** Credit balance: if k is greater than e, enter the difference . . . . — 6038
- **m** Funding deficiency: if e is greater than k, enter the difference . . . .

10 Alternative minimum funding standard account (omit if not used):
- **a** Was the entry age normal cost method used to determine entries in item 9 above? . . . . ☐ Yes ☐ No
  If "No," do not complete b through h.
- **b** Prior year alternate funding deficiency, if any . . . .
- **c** Normal cost . . . .
- **d** Excess, if any, of value of accrued benefits over market value of assets . . . . .
- **e** Interest on b, c, and d . . . .
- **f** Employer contributions (total from column (b) of item 7) . . . .
- **g** Interest on f . . . .
- **h** Funding deficiency: if the sum of b through e is greater than the sum of f and g, enter difference . . .

11 Actuarial cost method used as the basis for this plan year's funding standard account computation:
- **a** ☐ Attained age normal
- **b** ☐ Entry age normal
- **c** ☐ Accrued benefit (unit credit)
- **d** ☐ Aggregate
- **e** ☐ Frozen initial liability
- **f** ☐ Individual level premium
- **g** ☐ Other (specify) ▶

12 Checklist of certain actuarial assumptions:

	A Used for item 6d and e— value of accrued benefits				B Used for item 8, 9 or 10— funding standard account			
	Pre-retirement		Post-retirement		Pre-retirement		Post-retirement	
a Rates specified in insurance or annuity contracts.	☐ Yes	☐ No	☐ Yes	☐ No	☐ Yes	☐ No	☐ Yes	☐ No
b Mortality table code:								
(i) Males								
(ii) Females								
c Interest rate	%		%		%		%	
d Retirement age								
e Expense loading	%		%		%		%	
f Annual withdrawal rate:	Male	Female			Male	Female		
(i) Age 25	%	%			%	%		
(ii) Age 40	%	%			%	%		
(iii) Age 55	%	%			%	%		
g Ratio of salary at normal retirement to salary at:								
(i) Age 25					%	%		
(ii) Age 40					%	%		
(iii) Age 55					%	%		

h Is a statement of actuarial assumptions, actuarial funding method, etc., attached? . . . . ☐ Yes ☐ No

FIGURE 11–4

Schedule B (Form 5500) 1987		Page **2**
8 Funding standard account and other information:		
a Accrued liabilities as determined for funding standard account as of (enter date) ▶		
b Value of assets as determined for funding standard account as of (enter date) ▶		
c Unfunded liability for spread-gain methods with bases as of (enter date) ▶		
d *(i)* Actuarial gains or (losses) for period ending ▶		
(ii) Shortfall gains or (losses) for period ending ▶		
e Amount of contribution certified by the actuary as necessary to reduce the funding deficiency to zero, from 9m or 10h (or the attachment for 4b if required)		

9 Funding standard account statement for this plan year ending ▶ 12/31/89	
Charges to funding standard account:	
a Prior year funding deficiency, if any	0
b Employer's normal cost for plan year as of mo. _1_ day _1_ yr. _89_	5538
c Amortization charges	
(i) Funding waivers (outstanding balance as of mo. ..... day .... yr. ..... ▶ $ ....)	0
(ii) Other than waivers (outstanding balance as of mo. _1_ day _1_ yr. _89_ ▶ $ _129134_)	16089
d Interest as applicable to the end of the plan year on a, b, and c	1298
e Total charges (add a through d)	22925
Credits to funding standard account:	
f Prior year credit balance, if any	6038
g Employer contributions (total from column (b) of item 7)	28000
h Amortization credits (outstanding balance as of mo. ..... day ..... yr. ..... ▶ $ ....)	0
i Interest as applicable to end of plan year on f, g, and h	362
j Other (specify) ▶	0
k Total credits (add f through j)	34400
Balance:	
l Credit balance: if k is greater than e, enter the difference	11475
m Funding deficiency: if e is greater than k, enter the difference	

10 Alternative minimum funding standard account (omit if not used):	
a Was the entry age normal cost method used to determine entries in item 9 above?	☐ Yes ☐ No
If "No," do not complete b through h.	
b Prior year alternate funding deficiency, if any	
c Normal cost	
d Excess, if any, of value of accrued benefits over market value of assets	
e Interest on b, c, and d	
f Employer contributions (total from column (b) of item 7)	
g Interest on f	
h Funding deficiency: if the sum of b through e is greater than the sum of f and g, enter difference . . .	

11 Actuarial cost method used as the basis for this plan year's funding standard account computation:

a ☐ Attained age normal	**b** ☐ Entry age normal	**c** ☐ Accrued benefit (unit credit)
d ☐ Aggregate	**e** ☐ Frozen initial liability	**f** ☐ Individual level premium
g ☐ Other (specify) ▶		

12 Checklist of certain actuarial assumptions:	**A** Used for item 6d and e—value of accrued benefits				**B** Used for item 8, 9 or 10—funding standard account			
	Pre-retirement		Post-retirement		Pre-retirement		Post-retirement	
	☐ Yes	☐ No	☐ Yes	☐ No	☐ Yes	☐ No	☐ Yes	☐ No
a Rates specified in insurance or annuity contracts. . . .								
b Mortality table code:								
(i) Males								
(ii) Females								
c Interest rate . . .			%	%			%	%
d Retirement age . . .								
e Expense loading . .			%	%			%	%
f Annual withdrawal rate:	Male	Female			Male	Female		
(i) Age 25	%	%			%	%		
(ii) Age 40	%	%			%	%		
(iii) Age 55	%	%			%	%		
g Ratio of salary at normal retirement to salary at:								
(i) Age 25 . . .					%	%		
(ii) Age 40 . . .					%	%		
(iii) Age 55 . . .					%	%		
h Is a statement of actuarial assumptions, actuarial funding method, etc., attached?							☐ Yes	☐ No

FIGURE 11–5

Schedule B (Form 5500) 1987   Page **2**

8 Funding standard account and other information:

  a Accrued liabilities as determined for funding standard account as of (enter date) ▶ ....

  b Value of assets as determined for funding standard account as of (enter date) ▶ ....

  c Unfunded liability for spread-gain methods with bases as of (enter date) ▶ ....

  d *(i)* Actuarial gains or (losses) for period ending ▶ ....

     (ii) Shortfall gains or (losses) for period ending ▶ ....

  e Amount of contribution certified by the actuary as necessary to reduce the funding deficiency to zero, from 9m or 10h (or the attachment for 4b if required) . . . .

9 Funding standard account statement for this plan year ending ▶ .... 12/31/88 ....

Charges to funding standard account:

a Prior year funding deficiency, if any	0
b Employer's normal cost for plan year as of mo. `1` day `1` yr. `88`	11820
c Amortization charges	
(i) Funding waivers (outstanding balance as of mo. ..... day ..... yr. ..... ▶ $ ....)	0
(ii) Other than waivers (outstanding balance as of mo. ..... day ..... yr. ..... ▶ $ ....)	0
d Interest as applicable to the end of the plan year on a, b, and c	709
e Total charges (add a through d)	12529

Credits to funding standard account:

f Prior year credit balance, if any	0
g Employer contributions (total from column (b) of item 7)	12000
h Amortization credits (outstanding balance as of mo. ..... day ..... yr. ..... ▶ $ ....)	0
I Interest as applicable to end of plan year on f, g, and h	720
j Other (specify) ▶	0
k Total credits (add f through j)	12720

Balance:

l Credit balance: if k is greater than e, enter the difference	191
m Funding deficiency: if e is greater than k, enter the difference	

10 Alternative minimum funding standard account (omit if not used):

  a Was the entry age normal cost method used to determine entries in item 9 above? . . . . ☐ Yes ☐ No

    If "No," do not complete b through h.

  b Prior year alternate funding deficiency, if any

  c Normal cost . . . .

  d Excess, if any, of value of accrued benefits over market value of assets

  e Interest on b, c, and d . . . .

  f Employer contributions (total from column (b) of item 7)

  g Interest on f . . . .

  h Funding deficiency: if the sum of b through e is greater than the sum of f and g, enter difference

11 Actuarial cost method used as the basis for this plan year's funding standard account computation:

  a ☐ Attained age normal   **b** ☐ Entry age normal   **c** ☐ Accrued benefit (unit credit)

  d ☐ Aggregate   **e** ☐ Frozen initial liability   **f** ☐ Individual level premium

  g ☐ Other (specify) ▶

12 Checklist of certain actuarial assumptions:

	A Used for item 6d and e— value of accrued benefits				B Used for item 8, 9 or 10— funding standard account			
	Pre-retirement		Post-retirement		Pre-retirement		Post-retirement	
	☐ Yes	☐ No	☐ Yes	☐ No	☐ Yes	☐ No	☐ Yes	☐ No
a Rates specified in insurance or annuity contracts . . .								
b Mortality table code:								
(i) Males								
(ii) Females								
c Interest rate	%		%		%		%	
d Retirement age								
e Expense loading . . .	%		%		%		%	
f Annual withdrawal rate:	*Male*	*Female*			*Male*	*Female*		
(i) Age 25	%	%			%	%		
(ii) Age 40	%	%			%	%		
(iii) Age 55	%	%			%	%		
g Ratio of salary at normal retirement to salary at:								
(i) Age 25					%	%		
(ii) Age 40					%	%		
(iii) Age 55					%	%		

  h Is a statement of actuarial assumptions, actuarial funding method, etc., attached? . . . . ☐ Yes ☐ No

FIGURE 11-6

Schedule B (Form 5500) 1987   Page **2**

8 Funding standard account and other information:
- **a** Accrued liabilities as determined for funding standard account as of (enter date) ▶ -----------------
- **b** Value of assets as determined for funding standard account as of (enter date) ▶ ------------------
- **c** Unfunded liability for spread-gain methods with bases as of (enter date) ▶ -----------------------
- **d** *(i)* Actuarial gains or (losses) for period ending ▶ ....
  (ii) Shortfall gains or (losses) for period ending ▶ ....
- **e** Amount of contribution certified by the actuary as necessary to reduce the funding deficiency to zero, from 9m or 10h (or the attachment for 4b if required) . . . .

9 Funding standard account statement for this plan year ending ▶ .... 12/31/89 ....

Charges to funding standard account:

a Prior year funding deficiency, if any	0
b Employer's normal cost for plan year as of mo. ..... day .... yr.	18547
c Amortization charges	
(i) Funding waivers (outstanding balance as of mo. ..... day .....yr. ..... ▶ $ ....)	0
(ii) Other than waivers (outstanding balance as of mo. ..... day .....yr. ..... ▶ $ ....)	0
d Interest as applicable to the end of the plan year on a, b, and c	1113
e Total charges (add a through d)	19660

Credits to funding standard account:

f Prior year credit balance, if any	191
g Employer contributions (total from column (b) of item 7)	19640
h Amortization credits (outstanding balance as of mo. ..... day ..... yr. ..... ▶ $ ....)	0
I Interest as applicable to end of plan year on f, g, and h	11
j Other (specify) ▶	0
k Total credits (add f through j)	19842

Balance:

l Credit balance: if k is greater than e, enter the difference	182
m Funding deficiency: if e is greater than k, enter the difference	

10 Alternative minimum funding standard account (omit if not used):
- **a** Was the entry age normal cost method used to determine entries in item 9 above? . . . . ☐ Yes ☐ No
  If "No," do not complete b through h.
- **b** Prior year alternate funding deficiency, if any . . . .
- **c** Normal cost . . . .
- **d** Excess, if any, of value of accrued benefits over market value of assets . . . .
- **e** Interest on b, c, and d . . . .
- **f** Employer contributions (total from column (b) of item 7) . . . .
- **g** Interest on f . . . .
- **h** Funding deficiency: if the sum of b through e is greater than the sum of f and g, enter difference . . .

11 Actuarial cost method used as the basis for this plan year's funding standard account computation:
- **a** ☐ Attained age normal   **b** ☐ Entry age normal   **c** ☐ Accrued benefit (unit credit)
- **d** ☐ Aggregate   **e** ☐ Frozen initial liability   **f** ☐ Individual level premium
- **g** ☐ Other (specify) ▶

12 Checklist of certain actuarial assumptions:

	A Used for item 6d and e— value of accrued benefits				B Used for item 8, 9 or 10— funding standard account			
	Pre-retirement		Post-retirement		Pre-retirement		Post-retirement	
	☐ Yes	☐ No	☐ Yes	☐ No	☐ Yes	☐ No	☐ Yes	☐ No
a Rates specified in insurance or annuity contracts. . . .								
b Mortality table code:								
(i) Males								
(ii) Females								
c Interest rate	%		%		%		%	
d Retirement age								
e Expense loading	%		%		%		%	
f Annual withdrawal rate:	*Male*	*Female*			*Male*	*Female*		
(i) Age 25	%	%			%	%		
(ii) Age 40	%	%			%	%		
(iii) Age 55	%	%			%	%		
g Ratio of salary at normal retirement to salary at:								
(i) Age 25					%	%		
(ii) Age 40					%	%		
(iii) Age 55					%	%		

h Is a statement of actuarial assumptions, actuarial funding method, etc., attached? . . . . ☐ Yes ☐ No

FULL FUNDING LIMITATION

The full funding limitation is another concept that began with ERISA and then was amended by the Pension Protection Act of 1987. The full funding limitation limits the required contribution when the plan is considered fully funded. A related yet distinct purpose is to limit deductible contributions when the plan has sufficient assets. Because there are some distinctions in the two calculations, the calculation in a maximum deductible context is described in the next chapter.

The full funding limitation comes into play when the minimum end of year contribution according to the funding standard account exceeds the full funding limitation. Before the Pension Protection Act of 1987, the full funding limitation was defined as:

Accrued liability + Normal cost − (Assets − Credit balance)
+ Interest.

The accrued liability and normal cost are calculated according to the cost method in use if an immediate gain method is being used. For plans using a spread gain valuation method, the entry age normal method must be used. Assets are defined as the lesser of the actuarial and market value. Interest is to take all figures to the end of the plan year.

If this amount is less than the minimum contribution (exclusive of any credit balance), only that amount need be contributed. To prevent a deficiency in the funding standard account, a full funding credit equal to the difference between the minimum as defined and the full funding limitation would be credited. Due to the credit balance adjustment in the calculation, the plan's credit balance is preserved and increases with interest at the valuation rate.

In the year following a full funding credit, prior amortization bases are eliminated. New bases could be created in the subsequent year for an experience loss, plan amendments, or assumption changes. The loss is calculated as the sum of the credit balance plus any unfunded liability calculated according to the previous benefit formula and assumptions. Thus, in the following year, the minimum contribution is based on the normal cost, amortization of any new bases, as well as a possible reapplication of the full funding limitation. As of plan years beginning in 1988, an additional limit takes effect. This new limit and its implications are described in Chapter 13.

WAIVER OF MINIMUM FUNDING

Because some companies that sponsor defined benefit plans may be unable to make a contribution in a given year, waivers of minimum funding standards are available. The Internal Revenue Service may grant a waiver if it is in the best interest of the plan participants. The following factors are considered:

The employer is operating at an economic loss.

Unemployment in the employer's business and industry is substantial.

Sales or profits in the industry are depressed or declining.

The plan is unable to exist unless the waiver is granted.

The Pension Protection Act of 1987 added that the business hardship must be temporary in order to apply for a funding waiver. In addition, the waiver must be applied for within 2 1/2 months after the plan year end.

Waivers are limited to 3 out of any 15 consecutive years, and the amount waived must be amortized over 5 years, beginning with the year following the year in which the waiver was granted. (See Chapter 13 regarding the specific interest rates to be used for amortization of waivers.) Amortization of past waiver payments may not be waived in a future year. However, if a full funding limitation applies, the waived amount may be considered fully amortized, as discussed above. (However, see Chapter 13 for a further discussion on the 1987 act's effect on the full funding limitation.)

The minimum funding standard accounts in Figures 11–7 and 11–8 illustrate the application of a funding waiver (figures from Chapter 6).

The second year's normal cost is different from that calculated in Chapter 6. Under the waiver, no contribution was made in the first year, so the plan had no assets as of the end of the year. The normal cost was recalculated to compensate. The amortization amount would be calculated as follows:

$$\$12,529 / 4.465 = \$2,806.$$

It was assumed that a contribution of $24,108 was made on the last day of the plan year.

As mentioned above, a plan sponsor can apply for and receive a funding waiver in 3 out of any 15 consecutive years. Also, recall that

FIGURE 11–7
First Year of Waiver

Schedule B (Form 5500) 1987	Page **2**

8 Funding standard account and other information:
- **a** Accrued liabilities as determined for funding standard account as of (enter date) ▶ ....
- **b** Value of assets as determined for funding standard account as of (enter date) ▶ ....
- **c** Unfunded liability for spread-gain methods with bases as of (enter date) ▶ ....
- **d** *(i)* Actuarial gains or (losses) for period ending ▶ ....
  (ii) Shortfall gains or (losses) for period ending ▶ ....
- **e** Amount of contribution certified by the actuary as necessary to reduce the funding deficiency to zero, from 9m or 10h (or the attachment for 4b if required) . . . .

9 Funding standard account statement for this plan year ending ▶ 12/31/88 ....

Charges to funding standard account:
- **a** Prior year funding deficiency, if any . . . . — 0
- **b** Employer's normal cost for plan year as of mo. 1 day 1 yr. 88 . — 11820
- **c** Amortization charges
  - *(i)* Funding waivers (outstanding balance as of mo. .... day .... yr. .... ▶ $ ....) — 0
  - *(ii)* Other than waivers (outstanding balance as of mo. .... day .... yr. .... ▶ $ ....) — 0
- **d** Interest as applicable to end of the plan year on a, b, and c . . . — 709
- **e** Total charges (add a through d) . . . . — 12529

Credits to funding standard account:
- **f** Prior year credit balance, if any . . . — 0
- **g** Employer contributions (total from column (b) of item 7) . . . — 0
- **h** Amortization credits (outstanding balance as of mo. .... day .... yr. .... ▶ $ ....) — 0
- **i** Interest as applicable to end of plan year on f, g, and h . . . — 0
- **j** Other (specify) ▶ .... Waiver .... — 12529
- **k** Total credits (add f through j) . . . — 12529

Balance:
- **l** Credit balance: if k is greater than e, enter the difference . . . — 0
- **m** Funding deficiency: if e is greater than k, enter the difference . . . — 0

10 Alternative minimum funding standard account (omit if not used):
- **a** Was the entry age normal cost method used to determine entries in item 9 above? . . . . . . ☐ Yes ☐ No
  If "No," do not complete b through h.
- **b** Prior year alternate funding deficiency, if any . . .
- **c** Normal cost . . .
- **d** Excess, if any, of value of accrued benefits over market value of assets . . .
- **e** Interest on b, c, and d . . .
- **f** Employer contributions (total from column (b) of item 7) . . .
- **g** Interest on f . . .
- **h** Funding deficiency: if the sum of b through e is greater than the sum of f and g, enter difference . . .

11 Actuarial cost method used as the basis for this plan year's funding standard account computation:
- **a** ☐ Attained age normal **b** ☐ Entry age normal **c** ☐ Accrued benefit (unit credit)
- **d** ☐ Aggregate **e** ☐ Frozen initial liability **f** ☐ Individual level premium
- **g** ☐ Other (specify) ▶

12 Checklist of certain actuarial assumptions:

	A Used for item 6d and e— value of accrued benefits				B Used for item 8, 9 or 10— funding standard account			
	Pre-retirement		Post-retirement		Pre-retirement		Post-retirement	
a Rates specified in insurance or annuity contracts . .	☐ Yes	☐ No	☐ Yes	☐ No	☐ Yes	☐ No	☐ Yes	☐ No
b Mortality table code:								
(i) Males . . .								
(ii) Females . . .								
c Interest rate . .	%		%		%		%	
d Retirement age . .								
e Expense loading . .	%		%		%		%	
f Annual withdrawal rate:	Male	Female			Male	Female		
(i) Age 25 . .	%	%			%	%		
(ii) Age 40 . .	%	%			%	%		
(iii) Age 55 . .	%	%			%	%		
g Ratio of salary at normal retirement to salary at:								
(i) Age 25 . .					%	%		
(ii) Age 40 . .					%	%		
(iii) Age 55 . .					%	%		
h Is a statement of actuarial assumptions, actuarial funding method, etc., attached?				☐ Yes		☐ No		

FIGURE 11-8
Second Year of Waiver

Schedule B (Form 5500) 1987	Page 2

8 Funding standard account and other information:
   a Accrued liabilities as determined for funding standard account as of (enter date) ▶ ....
   b Value of assets as determined for funding standard account as of (enter date) ▶ ....
   c Unfunded liability for spread-gain methods with bases as of (enter date) ▶ ....
   d *(i)* Actuarial gains or (losses) for period ending ▶ ....
       (ii) Shortfall gains or (losses) for period ending ▶ ....
   e Amount of contribution certified by the actuary as necessary to reduce the funding deficiency to zero, from 9m or 10h (or the attachment for 4b if required) . . . .

9 Funding standard account statement for this plan year ending ▶ ....

Charges to funding standard account:

a	Prior year funding deficiency, if any	0
b	Employer's normal cost for plan year as of mo. ..... day ..... yr.	19937
c	Amortization charges	
	(i) Funding waivers (outstanding balance as of mo. ..... day ..... yr. ..... ▶ $ ....)	2806
	(ii) Other than waivers (outstanding balance as of mo. ..... day ..... yr. ..... ▶ $ ....)	0
d	Interest as applicable to the end of the plan year on a, b, and c	1365
e	Total charges (add a through d)	24108

Credits to funding standard account:

f	Prior year credit balance, if any	0
g	Employer contributions (total from column (b) of item 7)	24108
h	Amortization credits (outstanding balance as of mo. ..... day ..... yr. ..... ▶ $ ....)	0
i	Interest as applicable to end of plan year on f, g, and h	0
j	Other (specify) ▶	0
k	Total credits (add f through j)	24108

Balance:

l	Credit balance: if k is greater than e, enter the difference	0
m	Funding deficiency: if e is greater than k, enter the difference	0

10 Alternative minimum funding standard account (omit if not used):
   a Was the entry age normal cost method used to determine entries in item 9 above? . . . . ☐ Yes ☐ No
       If "No," do not complete b through h.
   b Prior year alternate funding deficiency, if any . . . .
   c Normal cost . . . .
   d Excess, if any, of value of accrued benefits over market value of assets . . . .
   e Interest on b, c, and d . . . .
   f Employer contributions (total from column (b) of item 7) . . . .
   g Interest on f . . . .
   h Funding deficiency: if the sum of b through e is greater than the sum of f and g, enter difference . . .

11 Actuarial cost method used as the basis for this plan year's funding standard account computation:
   a ☐ Attained age normal   **b** ☐ Entry age normal   **c** ☐ Accrued benefit (unit credit)
   d ☐ Aggregate   **e** ☐ Frozen initial liability   **f** ☐ Individual level premium
   g ☐ Other (specify) ▶

12 Checklist of certain actuarial assumptions:

		A Used for item 6d and e— value of accrued benefits				B Used for item 8, 9 or 10— funding standard account			
		Pre-retirement		Post-retirement		Pre-retirement		Post-retirement	
a	Rates specified in insurance or annuity contracts. . . .	☐ Yes	☐ No	☐ Yes	☐ No	☐ Yes	☐ No	☐ Yes	☐ No
b	Mortality table code:								
	(i) Males								
	(ii) Females								
c	Interest rate	%		%		%		%	
d	Retirement age								
e	Expense loading	%		%		%		%	
f	Annual withdrawal rate:	*Male*	*Female*			*Male*	*Female*		
	(i) Age 25	%	%			%	%		
	(ii) Age 40	%	%			%	%		
	(iii) Age 55	%	%			%	%		
g	Ratio of salary at normal retirement to salary at:								
	(i) Age 25					%	%		
	(ii) Age 40					%	%		
	(iii) Age 55					%	%		
h	Is a statement of actuarial assumptions, actuarial funding method, etc., attached? . . . . ☐ Yes ☐ No								

an amortization amount from a previous waiver cannot be waived. To illustrate, let's assume the plan sponsor wants to waive the maximum possible in the second year as well. As shown in the minimum funding standard account in Figure 11–9, the sponsor would have to contribute at least $2,975 ($2,806 × 1.06). The second waiver could be for up to $21,133. The total amortization charge in the third year would be calculated as follows:

$$(\$21,133 / 4.465) + 2,806 = \$7,539.$$

It is highly unlikely that a plan sponsor would set up a plan and receive a waiver of funding for the first two years.

EXTENSION OF AMORTIZATION PERIODS

Under a funding method with a supplemental liability, the plan sponsor has another option for coping with economically bad times. An extension of the amortization period for the unfunded past service liability can be obtained. To obtain an extension, the plan sponsor must prove plan participants will be protected and (as set forth in Internal Revenue Code Section 412(e)) failure to permit such extension would:

(1) Result in—
    (A) a substantial risk to the voluntary continuation of the plan, or
    (B) a substantial curtailment of pension benefit levels or employee compensation, and
(2) be adverse to the interests of plan participants in the aggregate.

The extension can be for up to 10 years. Therefore, supplemental liabilities could be amortized over 40 rather than 30 years. To illustrate, consider the supplemental liability calculated in Chapter 4 under the entry age normal funding method:

Supplemental liability = $84,093.
Amortization over 30 years: $5,763.
Amortization over 40 years: $5,273.

With small numbers such as our example, the difference is not significant. However, under plans with large supplemental liabilities, an extension could help a plan sponsor.

FIGURE 11–9

Schedule B (Form 5500) 1987		Page **2**

8 Funding standard account and other information:

  a Accrued liabilities as determined for funding standard account as of (enter date) ▶ .... _____

  b Value of assets as determined for funding standard account as of (enter date) ▶ .... _____

  c Unfunded liability for spread-gain methods with bases as of (enter date) ▶ .... _____

  d *(i)* Actuarial gains or (losses) for period ending ▶ .... _____

     (ii) Shortfall gains or (losses) for period ending ▶ .... _____

  e Amount of contribution certified by the actuary as necessary to reduce the funding deficiency to zero, from 9m or 10h (or the attachment for 4b if required) .... _____

9 Funding standard account statement for this plan year ending ▶ ....

Charges to funding standard account:

a Prior year funding deficiency, if any	0
b Employer's normal cost for plan year as of mo. _____ day _____ yr. _____	19937
c Amortization charges	
(i) Funding waivers (outstanding balance as of mo. _____ day _____ yr. _____ ▶ $ ....)	2806
(ii) Other than waivers (outstanding balance as of mo. _____ day _____ yr. _____ ▶ $ ....)	0
d Interest as applicable to the end of the plan year on a, b, and c	1365
e Total charges (add a through d)	24108

Credits to funding standard account:

f Prior year credit balance, if any	0
g Employer contributions (total from column (b) of item 7)	2974
h Amortization credits (outstanding balance as of mo. _____ day _____ yr. _____ ▶ $ ....)	0
i Interest as applicable to end of plan year on f, g, and h	0
j Other (specify) ▶ .... waiver	21134
k Total credits (add f through j)	24108

Balance:

  l Credit balance: if k is greater than e, enter the difference ....

  m Funding deficiency: if e is greater than k, enter the difference

10 Alternative minimum funding standard account (omit if not used):

  a Was the entry age normal cost method used to determine entries in item 9 above? .... ☐ Yes ☐ No

    If "No," do not complete b through h.

  b Prior year alternate funding deficiency, if any ....

  c Normal cost ....

  d Excess, if any, of value of accrued benefits over market value of assets ....

  e Interest on b, c, and d ....

  f Employer contributions (total from column (b) of item 7) ....

  g Interest on f ....

  h Funding deficiency: if the sum of b through e is greater than the sum of f and g, enter difference ....

11 Actuarial cost method used as the basis for this plan year's funding standard account computation:

  a ☐ Attained age normal   **b** ☐ Entry age normal   **c** ☐ Accrued benefit (unit credit)

  d ☐ Aggregate   **e** ☐ Frozen initial liability   **f** ☐ Individual level premium

  g ☐ Other (specify) ▶

12 Checklist of certain actuarial assumptions:

	A Used for item 6d and e— value of accrued benefits				B Used for item 8, 9 or 10— funding standard account			
	Pre-retirement		Post-retirement		Pre-retirement		Post-retirement	
a Rates specified in insurance or annuity contracts.	☐ Yes	☐ No	☐ Yes	☐ No	☐ Yes	☐ No	☐ Yes	☐ No
b Mortality table code:								
(i) Males								
(ii) Females								
c Interest rate	%		%		%		%	
d Retirement age								
e Expense loading	%		%		%		%	
f Annual withdrawal rate:	Male	Female			Male	Female		
(i) Age 25	%	%			%	%		
(ii) Age 40	%	%			%	%		
(iii) Age 55	%	%			%	%		
g Ratio of salary at normal retirement to salary at:								
(i) Age 25					%	%		
(ii) Age 40					%	%		
(iii) Age 55					%	%		
h Is a statement of actuarial assumptions, actuarial funding method, etc., attached?							☐ Yes	☐ No

Under Code Section 412(f), a plan sponsor that obtains either an amortization extension or a funding waiver generally is prohibited from increasing benefits under the plan while the waiver or extension is in effect.

With the new shorter amortization periods and the new tougher requirements for obtaining a waiver, extensions could become more common. All bases except for waiver bases can be extended.

ALTERNATIVE MINIMUM FUNDING STANDARD ACCOUNT

ERISA also created the alternative minimum funding standard account. As the name indicates, it is an alternative to the regular minimum funding standard account. However, its use is generally limited to plans using the entry age normal cost funding method. (They must have switched to this method in the past five years.) When using the alternative minimum funding standard account, it is necessary to calculate the normal cost and present value of accrued benefits under the accrued benefit (unit credit) funding method, as well as doing all the standard calculations under the entry age normal funding method.

The alternative minimum funding standard account can be used to reduce the required contributions, if the present value of accrued benefits (see Chapter 8) is less than the value of the plan assets.

When the alternative minimum funding standard account is used, Part 10 of the Schedule B must be completed along with Part 9.

The normal cost shown in Part 10c is the lesser of the normal cost under the entry age normal cost method or the normal cost under the unit credit method.

To illustrate, let's assume the market value of the plan's assets was $62,800 (it is not allowable to use an actuarial value of assets), the normal cost was $5,780 under the entry age normal method and $12,510 under the unit credit method, and the present value of accrued benefits was $62,530. Part 10c would be $5,780 and Part 10d would be calculated as follows:

$$\$62,530 - 62,800 = \$(270).$$

As long as the contribution is at least $6,127 as of the last day of the plan year, the alternative minimum funding standard account would be satisfied. Note, however, that the regular minimum funding standard account may show a deficiency when using the alternative minimum funding standard account. The deficiency accumulates until there is a switch back to the regular minimum funding standard account. The deficiency amount at the time of switch back would be a credit. Then, this switchback credit would be amortized as a charge over five years, beginning with the year of the switchback.

Figures 11–10 and 11–11 illustrate Parts 9 and 10 of the Schedule B for the first time the alternative minimum funding standard account is used. For Part 9, assume a credit balance of zero, no amortization credits, and an amortizations charge of $2,370.

Assume the same entry age normal cost in the next year: $5,780. Assume also that the normal cost under the accrued benefit funding method is $13,260, the present value of accrued benefits are $66,290, and the assets are $74,000. Further assume the alternative minimum funding standard account is no longer used. Figure 11–12 shows how the minimum funding standard account would appear.

There is a switchback credit of $2,512 in the transition year. It is the deficiency in the regular minimum funding standard account due to use of the alternative minimum funding standard account. This switchback credit is amortized over five years as a charge to the minimum funding standard account. The amortization of the switchback credit is $563. With all previous assumptions, the next year's minimum funding standard account would appear as in Figure 11–13.

EFFECTS OF CHANGES IN ACTUARIAL ASSUMPTIONS AND FUNDING METHODS ON THE MINIMUM FUNDING STANDARD ACCOUNT

Actuarial Assumptions

As discussed in Chapter 10, it is often necessary or desirable to change actuarial assumptions. The effect of these changes on the minimum funding standard account depends on the funding method. For the aggregate and individual aggregate funding methods, the change in assumptions is reflected in the normal cost. However, a change in assumptions for the remaining funding methods requires a special

FIGURE 11-10

Schedule B (Form 5500) 1987		Page 2
8 Funding standard account and other information:		
a Accrued liabilities as determined for funding standard account as of (enter date) ▶		
b Value of assets as determined for funding standard account as of (enter date) ▶		
c Unfunded liability for spread-gain methods with bases as of (enter date) ▶		
d (i) Actuarial gains or (losses) for period ending ▶		
(ii) Shortfall gains or (losses) for period ending ▶		
e Amount of contribution certified by the actuary as necessary to reduce the funding deficiency to zero, from 9m or 10h (or the attachment for 4b if required)		
9 Funding standard account statement for this plan year ending ▶ 12/31/90		
Charges to funding standard account:		
a Prior year funding deficiency, if any		0
b Employer's normal cost for plan year as of mo. 1 day 1 yr. 90		5780
c Amortization charges		
(i) Funding waivers (outstanding balance as of mo. ___ day ___ yr. ___ ▶ $ ___)		0
(ii) Other than waivers (outstanding balance as of mo. 1 day 1 yr. 90 ▶ $ ___)		2370
d Interest as applicable to the end of the plan year on a, b, and c		489
e Total charges (add a through d)		8639
Credits to funding standard account:		
f Prior year credit balance, if any		0
g Employer contributions (total from column (b) of item 7)		6127
h Amortization credits (outstanding balance as of mo. ___ day ___ yr. ___ ▶ $ ___)		0
I Interest as applicable to end of plan year on f, g, and h		0
J Other (specify) ▶		0
k Total credits (add f through j)		6127
Balance:		
l Credit balance: if k is greater than e, enter the difference		0
m Funding deficiency: if e is greater than k, enter the difference		2512

FIGURE 11-11

10 Alternative minimum funding standard account (omit if not used):						
a Was the entry age normal cost method used to determine entries in item 9 above?					☒ Yes ☐ No	
If "No," do not complete b through h.						
b Prior year alternate funding deficiency, if any					0	
c Normal cost					5780	
d Excess, if any, of value of accrued benefits over market value of assets					0	
e Interest on b, c, and d					347	
f Employer contributions (total from column (b) of item 7)					6127	
g Interest on f					0	
h Funding deficiency: if the sum of b through e is greater than the sum of f and g, enter difference					0	

11 Actuarial cost method used as the basis for this plan year's funding standard account computation:		
a ☐ Attained age normal	b ☐ Entry age normal	c ☐ Accrued benefit (unit credit)
d ☐ Aggregate	e ☐ Frozen initial liability	f ☐ Individual level premium
g ☐ Other (specify) ▶		

12 Checklist of certain actuarial assumptions:	A Used for item 6d and e— value of accrued benefits				B Used for item 8, 9 or 10— funding standard account			
	Pre-retirement		Post-retirement		Pre-retirement		Post-retirement	
a Rates specified in insurance or annuity contracts	☐ Yes	☐ No	☐ Yes	☐ No	☐ Yes	☐ No	☐ Yes	☐ No
b Mortality table code:								
(i) Males								
(ii) Females								
c Interest rate	%		%		%		%	
d Retirement age								
e Expense loading	%		%		%		%	
f Annual withdrawal rate:	Male	Female			Male	Female		
(i) Age 25	%	%			%	%		
(ii) Age 40	%	%			%	%		
(iii) Age 55	%	%			%	%		
g Ratio of salary at normal retirement to salary at:								
(i) Age 25					%	%		
(ii) Age 40					%	%		
(iii) Age 55					%	%		
h Is a statement of actuarial assumptions, actuarial funding method, etc., attached?							☐ Yes	☐ No

FIGURE 11–12

Schedule B (Form 5500) 1987 — Page 2

8 Funding standard account and other information:
- **a** Accrued liabilities as determined for funding standard account as of (enter date) ▶ . . . .
- **b** Value of assets as determined for funding standard account as of (enter date) ▶ . . . .
- **c** Unfunded liability for spread-gain methods with bases as of (enter date) ▶ . . . .
- **d** *(i)* Actuarial gains or (losses) for period ending ▶ . . . .
  - *(ii)* Shortfall gains or (losses) for period ending ▶ . . . .
- **e** Amount of contribution certified by the actuary as necessary to reduce the funding deficiency to zero, from 9m or 10h (or the attachment for 4b if required) . . . .

9 Funding standard account statement for this plan year ending ▶ . . . . 12/31/91 . . . .

Charges to funding standard account:

a Prior year funding deficiency, if any	2512
b Employer's normal cost for plan year as of mo. ..... day ..... yr.	5780
c Amortization charges	
(i) Funding waivers (outstanding balance as of mo. ..... day ..... yr. ..... ▶ $ ....)	0
(ii) Other than waivers (outstanding balance as of mo. ..... day ..... yr. ..... ▶ $ ....)	2933
d Interest as applicable to the end of the plan year on a, b, and c	674
e Total charges (add a through d)	11899

Credits to funding standard account:

f Prior year credit balance, if any	0
g Employer contributions (total from column (b) of item 7)	9236
h Amortization credits (outstanding balance as of mo. ..... yr. ..... ▶ $ ....)	0
i Interest as applicable to end of plan year on f, g, and h	151
j Other (specify) ▶ .... Switchback Credit	2512
k Total credits (add f through j)	11899

Balance:
- **l** Credit balance: if k is greater than e, enter the difference . . . .
- **m** Funding deficiency: if e is greater than k, enter the difference . . .

10 Alternative minimum funding standard account (omit if not used):
- **a** Was the entry age normal cost method used to determine entries in item 9 above? . . . . ☐ Yes ☐ No
  If "No," do not complete b through h.
- **b** Prior year alternate funding deficiency, if any . . . .
- **c** Normal cost . . . .
- **d** Excess, if any, of value of accrued benefits over market value of assets . . . .
- **e** Interest on b, c, and d . . . .
- **f** Employer contributions (total from column (b) of item 7) . . . . .
- **g** Interest on f . . . .
- **h** Funding deficiency: if the sum of b through e is greater than the sum of f and g, enter difference . . .

11 Actuarial cost method used as the basis for this plan year's funding standard account computation:
- **a** ☐ Attained age normal   **b** ☐ Entry age normal   **c** ☐ Accrued benefit (unit credit)
- **d** ☐ Aggregate   **e** ☐ Frozen initial liability   **f** ☐ Individual level premium
- **g** ☐ Other (specify) ▶

12 Checklist of certain actuarial assumptions:

	A Used for item 6d and e— value of accrued benefits				B Used for item 8, 9 or 10— funding standard account			
	Pre-retirement		Post-retirement		Pre-retirement		Post-retirement	
	Yes	No	Yes	No	Yes	No	Yes	No
a Rates specified in insurance or annuity contracts. . . .	☐	☐	☐	☐	☐	☐	☐	☐
b Mortality table code:								
(i) Males								
(ii) Females								
c Interest rate.	%		%		%		%	
d Retirement age								
e Expense loading . . .	%		%		%		%	
f Annual withdrawal rate:	Male	Female			Male	Female		
(i) Age 25	%	%			%	%		
(ii) Age 40	%	%			%	%		
(iii) Age 55	%	%			%	%		
g Ratio of salary at normal retirement to salary at:								
(i) Age 25					%	%		
(ii) Age 40					%	%		
(iii) Age 55					%	%		

h Is a statement of actuarial assumptions, actuarial funding method, etc., attached? . . . . ☐ Yes ☐ No

FIGURE 11–13

Schedule B (Form 5500) 1987   Page **2**

8 Funding standard account and other information:
- **a** Accrued liabilities as determined for funding standard account as of (enter date) ▶ . . . .
- **b** Value of assets as determined for funding standard account as of (enter date) ▶ . . . .
- **c** Unfunded liability for spread-gain methods with bases as of (enter date) ▶ . . . .
- **d** *(i)* Actuarial gains or (losses) for period ending ▶ . . . .
  - *(ii)* Shortfall gains or (losses) for period ending ▶ . . . .
- **e** Amount of contribution certified by the actuary as necessary to reduce the funding deficiency to zero, from 9m or 10h (or the attachment for 4b if required) . . . .

9 Funding standard account statement for this plan year ending ▶   . . . . 12/31/92 . . . .

Charges to funding standard account:

a Prior year funding deficiency, if any	0
b Employer's normal cost for plan year as of mo. 1 day 1 yr. 92	5780
c Amortization charges	
(i) Funding waivers (outstanding balance as of mo. . . . . day . . . . yr. . . . . . ▶ $ . . . .)	0
(ii) Other than waivers (outstanding balance as of mo. . . . . day . . . . yr. . . . . . ▶ $ . . . .)	2933
d Interest as applicable to the end of the plan year on a, b, and c	523
e Total charges (add a through d)	9236

Credits to funding standard account:

f Prior year credit balance, if any	0
g Employer contributions (total from column (b) of item 7)	9236
h Amortization credits (outstanding balance as of mo. . . . . day . . . . yr. . . . . . ▶ $ . . . .)	0
i Interest as applicable to end of plan year on f, g, and h	0
j Other (specify) ▶	0
k Total credits (add f through j)	9236

Balance:

l Credit balance: if k is greater than e, enter the difference	0
m Funding deficiency: if e is greater than k, enter the difference	0

10 Alternative minimum funding standard account (omit if not used):
- **a** Was the entry age normal cost method used to determine entries in item 9 above? . . . . ☐ Yes ☐ No
  - If "No," do not complete b through h.
- **b** Prior year alternate funding deficiency, if any . . . .
- **c** Normal cost . . . .
- **d** Excess, if any, of value of accrued benefits over market value of assets . . . .
- **e** Interest on b, c, and d . . . .
- **f** Employer contributions (total from column (b) of item 7) . . . .
- **g** Interest on f . . . .
- **h** Funding deficiency: if the sum of b through e is greater than the sum of f and g, enter difference . . . . .

11 Actuarial cost method used as the basis for this plan year's funding standard account computation:
- **a** ☐ Attained age normal
- **b** ☐ Entry age normal
- **c** ☐ Accrued benefit (unit credit)
- **d** ☐ Aggregate
- **e** ☐ Frozen initial liability
- **f** ☐ Individual level premium
- **g** ☐ Other (specify) ▶

12 Checklist of certain actuarial assumptions:

	A Used for item 6d and e— value of accrued benefits				B Used for item 8, 9 or 10— funding standard account			
	Pre-retirement		Post-retirement		Pre-retirement		Post-retirement	
a Rates specified in insurance or annuity contracts. . . .	☐ Yes		☐ No	☐ Yes	☐ No	☐ Yes		☐ No	☐ Yes	☐ No
b Mortality table code:								
(i) Males								
(ii) Females								
c Interest rate	%		%		%		%	
d Retirement age								
e Expense loading . . .	%		%		%		%	
f Annual withdrawal rate:	Male	Female			Male	Female		
(i) Age 25	%	%			%	%		
(ii) Age 40	%	%			%	%		
(iii) Age 55	%	%			%	%		
g Ratio of salary at normal retirement to salary at:								
(i) Age 25					%	%		
(ii) Age 40					%	%		
(iii) Age 55					%	%		
h Is a statement of actuarial assumptions, actuarial funding method, etc., attached?							☐ Yes	☐ No

amortization amount. The difference between the unfunded liability before and after the change is amortized over 10 years.

Funding Methods

Changes in funding methods are covered under revenue procedures developed by the Internal Revenue Service. Changes in asset valuation methods and valuation dates are considered to be changes in funding methods. Revenue Procedure 85–29, as corrected by Announcement 85–82, is the latest procedure at this writing. Changes that comply with the procedure are automatically approved. All other changes require advance approval from the Internal Revenue Service.

If a funding method having amortization bases is changed to another funding method with amortization bases, the prior bases are maintained as usual. In addition, a funding method charge base, which could be either a charge or a credit base, is created. It is calculated under the following formula:

Unfunded accrued liability under new method − (Outstanding balance of existing bases − Credit balance) = Funding method charge base.

This charge is amortized as follows under Revenue Procedure 85–29 (which applies to funding method changes between January 1, 1984, and January 1, 1990).

. . . the amortization period is the greater of
(i) the excess, if any of (1) 40 years, if the plan was in existence on January 1, 1974, or 30 years if it was not then in existence over (2) the number of prior plan years for which section of the ERISA or section 412 of the Code applied, or
(ii) the lesser of 15 years or the weighted average future working lifetime of the active employees.

The second time period (ii) will never be applicable because the first period will always be greater until up to January 1, 1990.

If the amount to be amortized is a credit rather than a charge, the amortization period is 30 years.

When changing to a funding method that normally does not have amortization bases, such as to the aggregate or individual aggregate methods, only certain prior bases must be kept. These bases include the waiver and five-year switchback bases (and shortfall bases on collectively bargained plans). All other bases are considered fully amortized.

Bases are amounts being amortized, such as experience gains or losses, past service liability, waiver and switchback amounts, changes in liabilities due to amendments or changes in assumptions, shortfall amounts, and amounts due to a change in funding method. The above formula given for calculating the funding method change base is also known as the balance equation:

Net sum of existing bases − Credit balance (or + Debit balance) =
Unfunded liability.

The balance equation is used by the actuary or the Internal Revenue Service to make sure the Schedule B is in balance mathematically.

Reasons to change funding methods include:

To simplify calculations.
To allow more flexibility.
To increase or decrease current contributions
To simplify a change in actuarial service provider.

ACTUARIAL VALUATION OF ASSETS

Up to this point it has been assumed that assets have been valued at market value. This is acceptable, but not strictly necessary. The actuary can choose any method of asset valuation that meets certain basic requirements. The method must be applied consistently and can be changed only with IRS approval. The method also must reflect market value and cannot produce a value consistently above or below market value. It also must produce a value that is at least 80 percent but not more than 120 percent of market value.

An actuarial value is used in calculating normal cost under spread gain methods and experience gain or loss under immediate gain methods because fluctuations in market values can be smoothed over time. Consider a simple example where existing assets are 10 times the current normal cost. Assume the plan suffers a 5 percent decline in market value as opposed to assumed earnings of 5 percent. The plan would have an investment loss for the year equal to the normal cost. With five-year amortization of this loss, the effect on the total cost for the next five years would be significant.

While use of an actuarial value cannot mask real investment losses forever, an averaging process satisfying requirements smoothes any shocks over a longer period. Ideally, this allows for a neutralizing process as gains and losses offset each other. With shorter periods required for the amortization of experience losses, use of such smoothing techniques becomes more important.

OTHER MINIMUM FUNDING STANDARD ACCOUNT ISSUES

We have discussed only issues that are likely to arise in small defined benefit plans. Minimum funding standard accounts can be more complicated for larger plans. Some complicating issues include:

Use of the shortfall method for collectively bargained plans.

Use of more sophisticated assumptions and more frequent changes in assumptions.

Added provisions in the Pension Protection Act of 1987 for additional contributions to satisfy minimum funding standards for plans with unfunded current liabilities and unpredictable contingent events. These provisions are effective for plans with greater than 100 participants and are discussed in Chapter 13.

Students should consult Code Section 412 and regulations to further understand the more complicated minimum funding standard accounts.

CHAPTER 12

DEDUCTIBLE CONTRIBUTIONS AND CODE SECTION 404

OVERVIEW

As discussed in Chapter 11, defined benefit calculations are used in three major ways:

To determine the pension expense for financial statement purposes.

To determine whether the plan is properly funded.

To determine the deduction for income tax purposes.

Contributions made to a qualified pension or profit sharing plan are deductible as "ordinary and necessary expenses paid or incurred during the taxable year in carrying on any trade or business" under Section 162 of the Internal Revenue Code. This means contributions made by an employer to the trust help to reduce the tax burden of an employer. In this way, Congress encourages adoption and maintenance of private pensions in the United States. Many small employers adopt pension plans primarily for these tax advantages.

However, in order for a plan to be qualified and for the employer to get a deduction, complex rules must be followed. Most of these rules are set forth in various sections of the Internal Revenue Code, including Sections 401, 404, 410, 411, 412 (discussed in Chapter 11), 415, and 416. Code Section 401 addresses qualification issues; Section 410, participation; Section 411, vesting; and Section 416, "top-heavy" rules. Code Sections 404 and 415 are discussed in this chapter.

Code Section 404 covers rules on maximum deductions. The various types of plans have separate rules. The rules for defined benefit plans are covered under Code Section 404 (a)(1)(A) and are as follows:

(i) the amount necessary to satisfy the minimum funding standard provided by Section 412(a) for plan years ending within or with such taxable year (or for any prior plan year), if such amount is greater than the amount determined under clause (ii) or (iii) (whichever is applicable with respect to the plan).

(ii) the amount necessary to provide with respect to all of the employees under the trust the remaining unfunded cost of their past and current service credits distributed as a level amount, or a level percentage of compensation, over the remaining future service of each such employee, as determined under regulations prescribed by the Secretary, but if such remaining unfunded cost with respect to any 3 individuals is more than 50 percent of such remaining unfunded cost, the amount of such unfunded cost attributable to such individuals shall be distributed over a period of at least 5 taxable years.

(iii) an amount equal to the normal cost of the plan, as determined under regulations prescribed by the Secretary, plus, if past service or other supplementary pension or annuity credits are provided by the plan, an amount necessary to amortize the unfunded costs attributable to such credits in equal annual payments (until fully amortized) over 10 years, as determined under regulations prescribed by the Secretary.

The deductible amount can be further limited by the full funding limitation, as discussed in Chapter 11, when it is less than the amount determined under the regular calculations. However, the full funding calculation differs through a different asset adjustment than with the full funding calculation for minimum funding standards. Instead of subtracting the credit balance from the assets, undeducted contributions are subtracted.

The Pension Protection Act added a new rule for calculating deductible limits for plans with at least 100 participants. A deduction is allowed for a contribution amount equal to the unfunded current liability. (See Chapter 13 for discussion of the calculations of the current and unfunded current liability.) However, for the deduction limitation, excludable preparticipant service is not excluded, and the adjusted value of assets is determined without subtracting the credit balance.

CALCULATIONS

The maximum deduction calculation is done under the funding method in use for minimum funding standards. Generally, the individual aggregate and aggregate funding methods most closely follow clause (ii) above. The immediate gain and supplemental liability-type funding methods most closely follow clause (iii) above. Clause (i) is primarily a safeguard.

Example 1: Aggregate Funding Method

Under the aggregate funding method, the maximum deductible contribution is the normal cost (plus an interest adjustment when the calculations were done as of the first day of the plan year). Amounts used in this example are taken from Chapter 6. Note, however, that in practice, the asset adjustments made under the aggregate and the individual spread gain funding methods are done differently for deductibility purposes than for minimum funding purposes. As for calculation of the full funding limitation, assets are adjusted for undeducted contributions instead of for the credit balance.

Interest is calculated to the earlier of the last day of the plan year or the last day of the employer's fiscal year. Generally, an employer's fiscal year is the same as the plan year.

The calculation for the maximum deduction for the first plan year (assuming an identical fiscal year) under the aggregate funding method (see Chapter 6) would be as follows:

$$\$11,820 \times 1.06 = \$12,529.$$

It doesn't matter if the actual contribution date is before the plan year end.

For an example of the calculations for a fiscal year that does not coincide with the plan year, we will assume the plan year end is December 31 and the fiscal year end is June 30. Under Internal Revenue Code Regulation 1.404(a)-14(c), there are three choices for the deductible amount:

(1) The deductible limit determined for the plan year commencing within the taxable year.
(2) The deductible limit determined for the plan year ending within the taxable year, or
(3) A weighted average of alternatives (1) and (2). Such an average may be based, for example, upon the number of months of each plan year falling within the taxable year.
The employer must use the same alternative for each taxable year unless consent to change is obtained. . . .

Generally, choice (1) is used when the plan and fiscal years do not coincide. Therefore, in our example above, the taxable year ends six months before the plan year end, and only six months of interest is added.

$$\$11,820 + (11,820 \times .06 \times 6/12) = \$12,175.$$

Although an employer has 8½ months after the plan year end to make a contribution to satisfy minimum funding standards, the employer must make the contribution before the due date of its tax return, including extensions, for the contribution to be deductible.

Example 2: Entry Age Normal Funding Method

Deduction limits under funding methods with immediate gains or supplemental liabilities are calculated similarly to the minimum required contribution under the minimum funding standard account, but there are a few differences. Instead of amortizing supplemental liabilities (past service costs) over 30 or 40 years, 10-year amortization is allowed. The shorter duration of amortization allows for larger contributions than under the minimum funding standards. (Regulations under 1.404(a)-14 also allow for combining bases and a fresh-start alternative.)

To illustrate, we will use the calculations done in Chapter 4 for the entry age normal funding method. The maximum deductible contribution for the first plan year is the normal cost plus the 10-year amortization of the supplemental liability, adjusted for interest as discussed above.

$$
\begin{aligned}
\text{Normal cost} &= \$3,741. \\
\text{Past service liability} &= \$84,093. \\
\$84,093/7.802 &= \$10,778 \text{ (10-year amortization} \\
&\quad \text{at 6 percent).} \\
(3,741 + 10,778) \times 1.06 &= \$15,390 \\
&= \text{maximum deduction assuming} \\
&\quad \text{plan year and} \\
&\quad \text{fiscal year coincide.}
\end{aligned}
$$

Regulations for Code Section 404 describe the maintenance of bases after the initial year. Recall that bases are the amounts being amortized for such occurrences as experience gains or losses, changes in actuarial assumptions or funding methods, the past service liability, and other bases. Regulation 1.404(a)-14 (h)(3) provides that:

> For any plan year after the first year of a base, the unamortized amount of the base is equal to—
>
> (i) The unamortized amount of the base as of the valuation date in the prior plan year, plus
>
> (ii) Interest at the valuation rate from the valuation date in the prior plan year to the valuation date in the current plan year on the amount described in subdivision (i), minus
>
> (iii) The contribution described in paragraph (h)(4) of this section with respect to the base for the prior plan year.

Paragraph (h)(4) of these regulations describes the contribution allocated for the above paragraph.

> Contribution allocation with respect to each base. A portion of the total contribution for the prior plan year is allocated to each base. Generally, this portion equals the product of—
>
> (i) The total contribution described in paragraph (h)(6) of this section with respect to all bases, and
>
> (ii) The ratio of the amount described in paragraph (b)(3)(i) of this section with respect to the base to the sum (using true rather than absolute values) of such amounts with respect to all remaining bases.

Paragraph (h)(6) refers to the total deduction plus interest on the contributions for the prior year minus the normal cost plus interest for the prior year. Paragraph (b)(3)(i) is "the level annual amount necessary to amortize the base over 10 years using the valuation rate. . . ."

To put it simply, if the maximum allowable contribution is not made, you allocate to the bases the difference between the total contribution made and the amount necessary to satisfy normal cost. This amount is allocated between the existing bases in proportion to their amortization amounts.

MAXIMUM DEDUCTIONS AND CODE SECTION 415

Code Section 415 limits benefits and contributions available in qualified pension plans. Contributions under defined contribution plans are limited. Benefits are limited under defined benefit plans. All defined benefit plans of an employer are considered one plan for purposes of benefit limitations. The same holds true for all defined contribution plans of an employer. There are special limitations if an employer has both a defined contribution and a defined benefit plan.

Under a defined contribution plan, the sum of the employer contributions, employee contributions, and forfeitures cannot exceed the lesser of $30,000 or 25 percent of a participant's compensation for each year. For a defined benefit plan, the annual retirement benefit cannot exceed the lesser of $90,000 or 100 percent of compensation. The $90,000 has been indexed for cost of living and was $94,023 in 1988. The defined benefit percentage limit is based on the highest three-consecutive year average compensation. This percentage limit must be reduced pro rata if the participant has less than 10 years of service at retirement. The dollar limit must be reduced if any of the following situations occur:

> The participant has less than 10 years of participation at retirement.
>
> The normal retirement age under the plan is lower than the Social Security retirement age.
>
> The form of benefit is other than a life annuity or qualified joint and survivor annuity. (This reduction also applies to the percentage limit.)

If the normal retirement age is greater than the Social Security retirement age, the dollar limit can be increased. The Social Security retirement age is the age used as the retirement age under Section 216(l) of the Social Security Act. In the case of a plan participant who attains age 62 before January 1, 2000, this age is 65; for the participant who attains age 62 after December 31, 1999, and before January 1, 2017, 66; and for the participant who attains age 62 after December 31, 2016, age 67.

Suppose a plan participant with a three-year average compensation of $190,000 retires at his Social Security retirement age, and the plan benefit is a life annuity of 75 percent of average compensation. Seventy-five percent is less than 100 percent of compensation, so the percentage limit has not been exceeded. However, 75 percent of $190,000 is $142,500, and the dollar limit is exceeded. The maximum annual benefit this participant can receive is $90,000, as indexed, assuming 10 years of participation.

For purposes of both defined benefit and defined contribution plan calculations, compensation over $200,000 is ignored for top-heavy plans. For plan years beginning in 1989, compensation over $200,000 will be ignored for both non-top-heavy plans and top-heavy plans. For example, in 1989, if a defined contribution plan specifies that 5 percent of compensation must be contributed and the participant's compensation is $400,000, only 5 percent of $200,000 can be contributed for that participant (even though 5 percent of $400,000 is less than $30,000).

The dollar limitations on benefits, contributions, and compensation will eventually be increased for cost of living. However, the contribution and compensation increases won't occur until the defined benefit dollar limit is more than four times the defined contribution dollar limit.

As previously mentioned, if an employee participates in both a defined benefit and defined contribution plan of an employer, benefits or contributions must be further limited. A detailed discussion of two-plan limitations is too complex for an introductory text, but to simplify:

The sum of the defined benefit fraction and the defined contribution fraction must be less than or equal to 1.0. The fractions' numerators reflect actual benefits, and the denominators depend upon whether the dollar limits or percentage limits apply. If the percentage limit applies, the denominator is equal to 1.4 times the percentage limit. If the dollar limit applies, the denominator is 1.25 times the dollar limit. (For top-heavy plans with no extra minimum benefit, and for super top-heavy plans, 1.0 instead of 1.25 is used. See Internal Revenue Code Section 416 on top-heavy rules.)

Again, all defined benefit plans' benefits for one employer count as one defined benefit plan for the limitations. The same holds true for all defined contribution plans' contributions.

Example of Code Section 415 Limitations

For a simple example, assume a participant in both an employer's defined benefit and defined contribution plans makes $40,000. Assume the required contribution to the defined contribution plan is 10 percent of compensation. The maximum defined benefit is calculated as follows:

Step 1: Determine the contribution to the defined contribution plan. $40,000 × 0.10 = $4,000. This is the numerator to the defined contribution fraction.

Step 2: Determine the denominator to the defined contribution fraction. The denominator is the lesser of $30,000 × 1.25 or $40,000 × 0.25 × 1.4, or $14,000.

Step 3: Determine the defined contribution fraction. This is $4,000 / 14,000 = 0.285714.

Step 4: Determine the denominator to the defined benefit fraction. This is the lesser of $90,000 × 1.25 or $40,000 × 1.4, or $56,000.

Step 5: Determine defined benefit fraction. It is 1 minus the defined contribution fraction: $1 - 0.285714 = .714286$.

Step 6: Determine the numerator to the defined benefit fraction. Using algebra, $0.714286 = X / 56,000$. $X = 40,000$. Therefore, a defined benefit of 100 percent of compensation can be the retirement benefit.

In some cases, the defined contribution plan is limited, rather than the defined benefit plan as was shown in this example. In that situation, the defined benefit plan fraction is calculated first. Of course, the actual plan benefits may be lower than the Section 415 limitations, by plan formula.

The defined contribution fraction becomes more complex over the years because it is calculated on a cumulative basis. The lesser of 1.25 × the dollar limit and 0.25 × 1.4 × compensation is calculated each year. These amounts are then added for the denominator. The contributions and forfeitures for each year are added for the numerator.

A new requirement also limits employer deductions to the lesser of 25 percent of participants' compensation or the minimum funding requirement for the defined benefit plan when both a defined benefit and defined contribution plan exist.

Code Section 415 is discussed in this chapter because only contributions for benefits that satisfy the provisions of Section 415 can be deducted by the employer. Most defined benefit plans are written to limit benefits to satisfy these provisions.

CHAPTER 13

OVERVIEW OF THE PENSION PROTECTION ACT OF 1987 REQUIREMENTS FOR MINIMUM FUNDING STANDARDS

OVERVIEW

The Pension Protection Act is part of the 1987 Omnibus Budget Reconciliation Act. This act was an attempt by Congress to strengthen funding of pension plans. Congress believed many plan sponsors had been increasing benefits under their plans without adequately funding these increases. Also, some plan sponsors were using their plans to provide benefits to ease the strain of plant shutdowns and work force reductions.

The previous chapters covered Pension Protection Act requirements as they affect small plans (defined as plans with less than 100 participants). In this chapter, we will look at some of the new provisions that affect larger plans as well as review the act's provisions affecting all plans. Since at the time of this writing there are no regulations or other government interpretations of the new rules, I have simplified the illustrations and definitions. The student should follow the Internal Revenue Service interpretations when they are made available.

SUMMARY OF PENSION PROTECTION ACT REQUIREMENTS FOR ALL SIZE PLANS

- Amortization of actuarial gains or losses must be over a period of five years. The previous requirement was 15 years. For example, if an actuarial loss was $30,000 and the interest rate was 6 percent, 15-year amortization would have resulted in a funding standard account charge of $2,914. The five-year amortization charge is $6,719.

- Amortization of assumption changes must be over a period of 10 years. The previous requirement was 30 years.
- Amortization of funding waivers must be over a period of five years. The previous requirement was 15 years. Waivers may be granted in three years of any 15-year period. Previously, waivers could have been granted in five years of any 15-year period. Note that waivers granted before 1988 are not counted for determining the possible three years. Funding waiver amortization periods cannot be extended.
- The interest rate to be used for amortizing funding waivers and extensions of amortization is now specified. The rate is the greater of:

1. 150 percent of the federal mid-term rate in effect under Code Section 1274 for the first month of the plan year, or
2. The rate being utilized for plan valuation purposes.

The rate is redetermined each year. The Chapter 11 examples used the plan valuation interest rate. This rate was assumed to be greater for purposes of simplicity. In actual experience, it is currently likely the other rate will be higher.

- For plan years beginning in 1989, quarterly contributions are required. The quarterly contribution is based on the smaller of:

1. 100 percent of the minimum required amount for the prior plan year, or
2. 90 percent of the minimum for the current plan year.

Quarterly contribution requirements will be phased in over four years. During the phase-in years, the quarterly payments would be the following percentages of the proper base amount:

1989	6.25 percent
1990	12.50 percent
1991	18.75 percent
1992	25.00 percent

For example, if the minimum required amount for the prior plan year was $20,000 and for 1989 was $30,000, each quarterly payment in 1989 would be calculated as follows:

$$(\$30,000 \times 90 \text{ percent}) = \$27,000$$

Therefore, $20,000 is the smaller amount. Then, $20,000 × 6.25 percent = $1,250.

- As mentioned in Chapter 10, the Pension Protection Act specifies that each actuarial assumption must be reasonable on its own (explicit assumptions), or the implicit assumptions used must produce a contribution equivalent to the contribution produced if explicit assumptions were used. In addition, certain interest rates based on 30-year Treasury notes must be used in calculating the current liability.
- The method of calculating the full funding limitation was changed by the Pension Protection Act, as discussed in Chapter 11. The full funding limitation for years beginning in 1988 is the lesser of:

1. (Accrued liability + Normal cost) − Assets, or
2. 150 percent of the Current liability − (Assets − Credit balance).

You must use an interest rate based on 30-year Treasury notes for calculating the current liability.

If the 150 percent of current liability is lower, special rules apply. First, all amortizable amounts are not considered fully amortized, as they are when the other formula is applied. Also, the Internal Revenue Service may allow skipped contributions to be made up in later years.

Although the Pension Protection Act was generally supposed to increase funding, the new full funding limitation will probably decrease contributions to many small plans.

Figure 13–1 illustrates the new two-part calculation of the full funding limitation for a typical small plan that has been in existence for a number of years.

Implications of the New Full Funding Limit

Many plans are subject to a reduced full funding limit based upon 150 percent of the current liability. There are three potential reasons 150

FIGURE 13–1

Actuarial Valuation for Sample Small Company, Inc. Defined Benefit Pension Plan for the Plan Year 01/01/88 through 12/31/88

A. Valuation as of 01/01/88
   1. Present value of benefits $360,067.00
      A. Active   357,297.00
      B. Retired   0.00
      C. Deferred vested   2,770.00
   2. Assets   221,342.59
   3. Credit balance (funding deficiency)   0.00
   4. Present value of future normal cost (1 - (2 - 3))   138,724.41
   5. Normal cost   18,606.00

The normal cost amounts shown were calculated under the individual aggregate funding method. A 7% interest assumption was used for funding. The annuity purchase rate was based on the UP84 unisex table at 5%. A 1% salary scale was used. An 8.33% interest rate was used for calculating the current liability.

B. Full funding limitation
   1. A. Entry age accrued liability $295,062.00
      B. Entry age normal cost   7,352.00
      C. Net Premiums   0.00
   2. Assets—Credit balance   221,342.59
   3. Interest to end of year   5,675.00
   4. Section 412 full funding limitation 1 (not less than zero)   86,746.41
   5. 150% limit (1.5 * Current liability at end of year)   175,574.00
   6. Assets—Credit balance   221,342.59
   7. Interest on item 6 to end of year   15,493.99
   8. Section 412 full funding limitation 2 (not less than zero)   0.00
   9. Section 412 full funding limitation (lesser of 4 and 8)   0.00

percent of the current liability may be less than the accrued liability of the plan:

1. The current liability is based upon benefits currently accrued on a termination basis, while if benefits are pay-related, the accrued liability will reflect expected pay increases. This effect increases the younger the plan population is.

2. The entry age normal funding method naturally builds up an accrued liability in excess of a termination liability even if benefits are not pay related because the method levels the normal cost over time.

3. The statutory valuation rate used in the calculation of the current liability could exceed the valuation rate used in calculation of the plan's accrued liability.

Generally, plans with benefits based on final earnings and plans with younger participants are more likely to be subject to the current liability limitation than one based on the cost method used in valuation (or entry age normal funding method if applicable). In these cases, the ratio of the projected liability to the current liability on a termination basis is greatest.

The limit has two fundamental effects if the current value of adjusted assets is in excess of the limit; the minimum required but also the maximum deductible contribution would be zero. With a 10 percent excise tax for contributions above the currently deductible limit, funding for any plan subject to the limit is frozen as long as the adjusted value of plan assets exceeds 150 percent of the current liability.

The new limit may be desirable for those sponsors wishing access to plan surplus without plan termination. In the past, a complete suspension of contributions without termination could be achieved only in the following circumstances: through a very large credit balance, use of a waiver, if the old full funding limitation applied, or through a switch to the alternative funding standard account. Limitation of the alternative account to entry age normal plans and use of market value of assets in the calculation of charges restrict use of this option. Under the new limit, the sponsor can suspend contributions as long as the plan is in surplus as defined. Thus, if an objective of the new limit is to allow plan sponsors to recover surplus over time through suspended funding while the plan continues in existence, this is achievable.

The limit, however, also prevents contributions for those sponsors wishing to continue to contribute. Plan sponsors may wish to maintain contributions because of the tax motivations of current deductibility and tax sheltered accrual of plan assets as well as a possible desire to maintain an actual contribution as long as an accounting expense is being accrued.

Plans initially subject to the limit continue to accrue charges to their funding standard accounts because contributions suspended due to the new limit are only deferred. If the plan continues, the value of plan assets eventually falls below both funding limits in normal circumstances. The sponsor then is forced to make a contribution based upon the charges deferred while subject to the limit. In all likelihood, the contribution necessary to bring the plan to full funding based upon 150 percent of the current liability is less. In effect, plans could become perpetually subject to the limit, in which case they will ultimately be funded on an accrued benefit basis defined by the increase of 150 percent of the current liability from year to year.

A simple example will illustrate the constraining nature of the new limit. Consider a plan with a single employee, which begins at the employee's hire at age 25. The plan benefit is a one dollar lump sum, per year of service payable at age 65. In order to level costs, the entry age normal method, which in this example would be the same as the individual level premium method, is chosen for valuation.

In keeping with the principles of small plan valuation, mortality is ignored. The normal cost would be the projected benefit, which in this example is 40 divided by the accumulation factor $\ddot{s}_{\overline{40}|i}$, which would be defined by the plan's valuation rate. The accrued liability would equal the accumulated past normal costs, or normal cost times $\ddot{s}_{\overline{y-25}|i}$ where y is the attained age of the participant. The current liability, defined as 150 percent of the termination liability, would equal $(y-25) \times v^{65-y} \times 1.5$.

In this example, if a 6 percent valuation rate is assumed, 150 percent of the current liability will be less than the accrued liability according to the funding method for the first six years of operation. The implication would be that for the first six years of operation, the contribution that could be made would be defined by the increase in 150 percent of the current liability rather than by the plan's funding method. If extended to include a mortality decrement, the example would show the new limit below the old for the first 20 years of operation, again with a similar consequence.

A plan with a benefit based on final earnings would show an even longer period of application of the lower limit. The period would increase with the steepness of the salary progression assumption. The addition of new participants at young ages could mean this plan will become perpetually subject to the new limit, and application of a cost method would be moot because the plan would be perpetually funded based upon the increase in the current liability.

This funding phenomenon could ultimately have implications for plan design. Final average plans will be subject to the new limit when the participant group is young. This will prevent the accumulation of plan surplus. If the participant group ages, cost increases will be steep. Plan sponsors may wish to forgo such a risk through forgoing final average plans. Due to the ratio nature of the new limit, a lump sum distribution could bring a plan to a fully funded status. Consider a plan with $140,000 of assets and a current liability of $100,000. Assuming the current liability approximates the lump sum distribution to which a participant is entitled, a distribution of $20,000 would raise the funding ratio from 1.4 to 1.5. Lump sum distributions in defined benefit plans in all likelihood will become less common.

STRENGTHENED FUNDING REQUIREMENTS FOR PLANS WITH OVER 100 PARTICIPANTS

The Pension Protection Act requires an additional funding standard account charge. The purpose of this new charge is twofold. In the past, certain plans, especially those not based on final earnings, have been liberalized frequently and substantially, often including provisions for retroactive benefit increases. Under the prior law, increases in the accrued liability due to such amendments would have been charged to the funding standard account over a 30-year period. Under the new law, such increases will be amortized over a minimum of 18 years, with the rate of amortization increasing as the level of plan funding at the time of liberalization decreases. Plan sponsors will either have to increase the rate of funding or slow the rate of benefit liberalization.

The second charge will be directed toward those firms that have used their pension plan to solve business-related problems such as plant shutdown or work-force reduction. These situations have been termed as unpredictable contingent events under the new law if the benefits are both unpredictable and not contingent upon age, service, prior compensation, death, or disability. Firms have relied upon their pension funds to pay for severance benefits in these circumstances.

While such programs will not be prohibited under the new law, any increase in the plan's liability due to such events will have to be paid to the fund very rapidly.

Thus, the new additional charge will be the sum of an annual amortization charge to pay for benefit liberalizations and an unpredictable contingent event amount to pay for such an event if applicable. However, the total additional charge will not be more than is necessary to bring the plan to a fully funded status.

A plan is considered fully funded in this context if the adjusted value of assets, defined as the actuarial value minus any credit balance, exceeds the current liability. Incorporating all of these factors into a single equation and ignoring any interest will yield

Additional charge = minimum [(annual amortization charge
+ unpredictable contingent event amount),
(current liability − adjusted value of assets)].

CALCULATION OF THE ADDITIONAL FUNDING STANDARD ACCOUNT CHARGE

Up to now annual amortization charge, unpredictable contingent event amount, and current liability have not been precisely defined. We will begin by defining current liability.

Current Liability

This amount is defined as the value of all liabilities to participants and other beneficiaries, determined as if the plan were terminating. Thus, the amount is very close to the accrued liability that would be used if the alternative funding standard account were being used. However, there are certain differences. The current liability would be higher because it includes the value of any qualified preretirement survivor annuities, even when the participant is still alive. Early retirement subsidies must also be accounted for, although if they are contingent upon completion of a minimum period of service, only a proportion of the value must be recognized.

However, in determining current liability, certain years of service for certain participants can be excluded. For any qualifying participant with less than five years of participation, only a proportion of preparticipation service is included in calculating the current liability, for purposes of the new charge. This proportion begins at 20 percent after 1 year, increasing proportionately to the full 100 percent after 5 years. Thus, for a qualifying participant with 10 years of preparticipation service and 3 years of postparticipation service, 9 years of service would be counted. This would be made up of 60 percent of the preparticipation 10 and the full 3 years after. After 5 years of participation, the full 15 years of service would be counted. This special rule applies only to qualifying participants, defined as those who first become a participant in a plan year beginning after 1987, and who have not accrued any benefit under any other defined benefit plan in the controlled group.

Thus, a simplified representation of the current liability would be as follows: current liability = Present value of accrued benefits (on a termination basis) + Value of qualified preretirement survivor annuities + Part of the value of early retirement subsidies − Value of benefits attributable to excludable preparticipation service.

Annual Amortization Charge

The annual amortization charge equals the amount by which the deficit reduction amount exceeds the basic amortization amount or notationally:

Annual amortization charge = Deficit reduction amount − Basic amortization amount.

Basic Amortization Amount

The basic amortization amount is the net sum of the charges to the funding standard account for any initial unfunded liability and the charges for plan liberalizations minus any credits in the unlikely case there have been deliberalizations in the past. These are calculated through 30-year amortization of the bases created except for 40 years for any initial unfunded for a pre-ERISA plan.

Deficit Reduction Amount

The deficit reduction amount equals the sum of the unfunded old liability amount and the unfunded new liability amount, or

Deficit reduction amount = Unfunded old liability amount + Unfunded new liability amount;

thus,

Annual amortization charge = Unfunded old liability amount + Unfunded new liability amount − Basic amortization amount.

Unfunded Old Liability Amount

The unfunded old liability amount is the amount based upon 18-year amortization of any unfunded old liability and any unfunded existing benefit increase liability.

The unfunded old liability is defined as the unfunded current liability as of the beginning of the first plan year after 1988 except that plan amendments adopted after October 16, 1987, that increase liabilities are ignored. Thus,

Unfunded old liability = Current liability* − Adjusted value of
assets,

where current liability* indicates the calculation is based upon plan provisions as of October 16, 1987.

The unfunded existing benefit increase liability represents increases in the plan's accrued liability for plan years after 1988, due to collective bargaining agreements ratified before October 17, 1987. It is referred to as unfunded because it can be reduced if the adjusted value of plan assets exceeds the current liability as calculated, before reflection of these benefits. Thus, these future increases are treated effectively as old liabilities for funding standard account purposes. Thus we have:

Unfunded old liability amount = (Current liability* − Adjusted value
of assets + Unfunded existing benefit
increase liability) × amortization
factor,

where the amortization factor is for 18 years.

Unfunded New Liability Amount

The unfunded new liability amount is a certain percentage of the unfunded new liability. The unfunded new liability is defined as the unfunded current liability minus the unamortized unfunded old liability minus any unpredictable contingent events benefits liability for which the event has already occurred. As any unpredictable contingent event benefits for which the event has *not* occurred were already excluded, no such benefits enter into the calculation of the first additional charge, and all are handled in the unpredictable contingent event amount. This leaves the value:

Unfunded new liability = Current liability − Adjusted value of assets − Unamortized unfunded old liability − Unpredictable contingent event benefit liability.

In the first plan year after 1988, the unamortized unfunded old liability will be the full unfunded old liability and the calculation will reduce to:

Unfunded new liability = Current liability − Current liability* − Unpredictable contingent event benefit liability, where current liability* indicates the calculation is based upon plan provisions as of October 16, 1987.

The appropriate percentage is determined by the ratio of the funded current liability percentage defined as the ratio of the adjusted value of assets to the current liability:

Funded current liability percentage = minimum [1, (adjusted value of assets/current liability)].

The percentage is a maximum at 30 when funded current liability percentage is less than 35 percent. There is a decrease in the percentage of .25 percent for each 1 percent increase in the funded percentage. When this factor is greater than one signifying full funding, the amortization percentage decreases to 13.75 percent. Therefore,

Unfunded new liability amount = Unfunded new liability × Percentage = (Current liability − Adjusted value of assets − Unamortized unfunded old liability − Unpredictable contingent event benefit liability) × Percentage.

Example of Calculation of Annual Amortization Charge

Summarizing the charges for the annual amortization charge yields:

Annual amortization charge = Deficit reduction amount − Basic amortization amount = Unfunded old liability amount + Unfunded new liability amount − Basic amortization amount = (Current liability* −

Adjusted value of assets + Unfunded
existing benefit increase liability) ×
Amortization factor + (Current
liability − Adjusted value of assets
− Unamortized unfunded old liability
− Unpredictable contingent event
benefit liability) × Percentage −
Basic amortization amount.

Assuming the following plan characteristics:

Plan year: 1989.

Plan has more than 150 participants. Interest rate in calculation and amortization = 8½ percent (this rate must be calculated according to prescribed procedures).

Plan year is the same as calendar year.

A plan amendment was adopted between October 16, 1987, and January 1, 1989. Figures are as of January 1, 1989.

Current liability based upon plan provisions October 16, 1987: $2,250,000.

Current liability based upon plan provisions January 1, 1989: $2,500,000.

Assets: $2,000,000.

Credit balance: 0.

Adjusted asset value: $2,000,000.

Basic amortization amount: $45,000.

Unfunded existing benefit increase liability: $50,000.

Unpredictable contingent event benefit liability: $100,000.

Because it is the first year of the charge, the unamortized unfunded old liability will equal the initial unfunded old liability which is current liability* minus adjusted value of assets plus unfunded existing benefit increase liability. The interest rate of 8½ percent and the amortization period of 18 years will define the amortization factor for the unfunded old liability as .10178. All that is necessary is to calculate the percentage for amortization of the unfunded new liability.

In our example, the adjusted value of assets is $2,000,000, and the current liability is $2,500,000. Therefore, adjusted value of assets/current liability, which is termed the funded percentage, is 80 percent. Applying the formula percentage = 30 − (Funded percentage − 35) × .25, for any funded percentage greater than 35 but less than 100, yields $30 - 11.25 = 18.75$, or expressed in decimal notation percentage $= .1875$.

Incorporating all of the factors into a single equation yields:

$$
\begin{aligned}
\text{Annual amortization charge} &= (2{,}250{,}000 - \$2{,}000{,}000 + \\
&\quad \$50{,}000) \times .10178 + (\$2{,}500{,}000 \\
&\quad - \$2{,}000{,}000 - \$250{,}000 - \\
&= \$100{,}000) \times .1875 - \$45{,}000 \\
&= \$30{,}534 + \$28{,}125 - \$45{,}000 \\
&\quad \$13{,}659.
\end{aligned}
$$

This is the new funding standard account charge before calculation of the unpredictable contingent event amount.

Unpredictable Contingent Event Amount

The unpredictable contingent event amount is equal to the greater of:

1. Amortization over seven years of the value of the unpredictable contingent event benefits.
2. A percentage of the value of the unpredictable contingent event benefits actually paid in the plan year, including annuity premiums on annuities that cannot be liquidated. This amount is often referred to as a cash flow amount. The charge would be calculated as follows:

Cash flow $\times$ (100 $-$ Current liability/Adjusted value of assets)
$-$ Percentage based on plan year.

The plan year percentage is determined by the following schedule:

Plan Years Beginning In	Applicable Percentage
1989–90	5
1991	10
1992	15
1993	20
1994	30
1995	40
1996	50
1997	60
1998	70
1999	80
2000	90
2001 and after	100

Assuming a benefit paid in the plan year 1989, based on an unpredictable contingent event of $100,000, the charge based on seven-year amortization at 8½ percent would be $18,006. The charge based on the second calculation, assuming the plan was 80% funded, would be:

$$\$100,000 \times (100 - 80)\% \times 5\% = \$1,000.$$

Therefore, the charge based upon the larger of the two amounts would be $18,006.

New Funding Standard Account Charge

The new charge is defined as the sum of the two charges but not more than is necessary to fully fund the plan. Because $500,000 would be required to fully fund the plan, the additional charge would be $18,006 + $13,659 = $31,665. For plans with less than 150 but more than 100 participants, this charge would grade linearly toward zero for a plan with 100 participants. Thus, a plan with 125 participants would have one half of the additional charge.

Subsequent Plan Year

A new calculation for the additional charge would be required in the subsequent year. The only factor that would remain the same would be the unfunded old liability. The amount charged, however, may differ if the valuation rate for the amortization charge that must be calculated according to statutory principles has changed.

In calculating the unfunded new liability amount, a valuation would be necessary to determine the current liability and adjusted value of assets, as well as any unpredictable contingent event benefit liability. The unamortized unfunded old liability would be less than the previous year's due to the past year's amortization.

The percent factor could change because it is calculated as a function of the plan year and the funded status. The basic amortization amount would be adjusted for any new base due to a plan amendment that would be amortized over 30 years.

Statutory Valuation Rates

Statutory valuation rates are prescribed for two purposes. Bases created through funding waivers as well as any base subject to a 10-year extension of its amortization period is amortized according to a rate that is the greater of:

1. 150 percent of the federal midterm rate in effect for the first month of the plan year, or
2. The rate being utilized for plan valuation purposes.

This rate is predetermined each year for the existing waivers and extensions. The normal case is that 150 percent of the midterm rate exceeds the plan's rate. The use of a higher valuation rate increases the amortization charges relative to a lower rate.

The second statutory rate applies in calculating the new funding standard account charge and calculating the current liability in the determination of the new full funding limitation. This valuation rate must fall within a corridor of 90 percent and 110 percent of a 4-year average of 30-year Treasury Bill rates. This in itself is not sufficient because the rate must also be consistent with rates implicit in insurance company annuities, inclusive of expense charges. Dual valuation rates therefore are required unless the actuary prefers to tie the basic valuation rate to the statutory rate.

APPENDIX 1

INTEREST AND COMMUTATION TABLES

APPENDIX 1–A(1)
Present Value of One Dollar

Years				Interest Rates				
	.05000	.05500	.06000	.06500	.07000	.07500	.08000
1	.95238	.94787	.94340	.93897	.93458	.93023	.92593
2	.90703	.89845	.89000	.88166	.87344	.86533	.85734
3	.86384	.85161	.83962	.82785	.81630	.80496	.79383
4	.82270	.80722	.79209	.77732	.76290	.74880	.73503
5	.78353	.76513	.74726	.72988	.71299	.69656	.68058
6	.74622	.72525	.70496	.68533	.66634	.64796	.63017
7	.71068	.68744	.66506	.64351	.62275	.60275	.58349
8	.67684	.65160	.62741	.60423	.58201	.56070	.54027
9	.64461	.61763	.59190	.56735	.54393	.52158	.50025
10	.61391	.58543	.55839	.53273	.50835	.48519	.46319
11	.58468	.55491	.52679	.50021	.47509	.45134	.42888
12	.55684	.52598	.49697	.46968	.44401	.41985	.39711
13	.53032	.49856	.46884	.44102	.41496	.39056	.36770
14	.50507	.47257	.44230	.41410	.38782	.36331	.34046
15	.48102	.44793	.41727	.38883	.36245	.33797	.31524
16	.45811	.42458	.39365	.36510	.33873	.31439	.29189
17	.43630	.40245	.37136	.34281	.31657	.29245	.27027
18	.41552	.38147	.35034	.32189	.29586	.27205	.25025
19	.39573	.36158	.33051	.30224	.27651	.25307	.23171
20	.37689	.34273	.31180	.28380	.25842	.23541	.21455
21	.35894	.32486	.29416	.26648	.24151	.21899	.19866

22	.34185	.30793	.27751	.25021	.22571	.20371	.18394
23	.32557	.29187	.26180	.23494	.21095	.18950	.17032
24	.31007	.27666	.24698	.22060	.19715	.17628	.15770
25	.29530	.26223	.23300	.20714	.18425	.16398	.14602
26	.28124	.24856	.21981	.19450	.17220	.15254	.13520
27	.26785	.23560	.20737	.18263	.16093	.14190	.12519
28	.25509	.22332	.19563	.17148	.15040	.13200	.11591
29	.24295	.21168	.18456	.16101	.14056	.12279	.10733
30	.23138	.20064	.17411	.15119	.13137	.11422	.09938
31	.22036	.19018	.16425	.14196	.12277	.10625	.09202
32	.20987	.18027	.15496	.13329	.11474	.09884	.08520
33	.19987	.17087	.14619	.12516	.10723	.09194	.07889
34	.19035	.16196	.13791	.11752	.10022	.08553	.07305
35	.18129	.15352	.13011	.11035	.09366	.07956	.06763
36	.17266	.14552	.12274	.10361	.08754	.07401	.06262
37	.16444	.13793	.11579	.09729	.08181	.06885	.05799
38	.15661	.13074	.10924	.09135	.07646	.06404	.05369
39	.14915	.12392	.10306	.08578	.07146	.05958	.04971
40	.14205	.11746	.09722	.08054	.06678	.05542	.04603
41	.13528	.11134	.09172	.07563	.06241	.05155	.04262
42	.12884	.10554	.08653	.07101	.05833	.04796	.03946

Factor = $(1 + $ interest rate$)$ to the negative power of the number of years can be written as: v^n, $(1+i)^{-n}$, or $\frac{1}{(1+i)^n}$.

APPENDIX 1-A(2)
Accumulation of One Dollar

Years	.050	.055	.060	.065	.070	.075	.080
				Interest Rates			
1	1.050	1.055	1.060	1.065	1.070	1.075	1.080
2	1.103	1.113	1.124	1.134	1.145	1.156	1.166
3	1.158	1.174	1.191	1.208	1.225	1.242	1.260
4	1.216	1.239	1.262	1.286	1.311	1.335	1.360
5	1.276	1.307	1.338	1.370	1.403	1.436	1.469
6	1.340	1.379	1.419	1.459	1.501	1.543	1.587
7	1.407	1.455	1.504	1.554	1.606	1.659	1.714
8	1.477	1.535	1.594	1.655	1.718	1.783	1.851
9	1.551	1.619	1.689	1.763	1.838	1.917	1.999
10	1.629	1.708	1.791	1.877	1.967	2.061	2.159
11	1.710	1.802	1.898	1.999	2.105	2.216	2.332
12	1.796	1.901	2.012	2.129	2.252	2.382	2.518
13	1.886	2.006	2.133	2.267	2.410	2.560	2.720
14	1.980	2.116	2.261	2.415	2.579	2.752	2.937
15	2.079	2.232	2.397	2.572	2.759	2.959	3.172
16	2.183	2.355	2.540	2.739	2.952	3.181	3.426
17	2.292	2.485	2.693	2.917	3.159	3.419	3.700
18	2.407	2.621	2.854	3.107	3.380	3.676	3.996
19	2.527	2.766	3.026	3.309	3.617	3.951	4.316
20	2.653	2.918	3.207	3.524	3.870	4.248	4.661

21	2.786	3.078	3.400	3.753	4.141	4.566	5.034
22	2.925	3.248	3.604	3.997	4.430	4.909	5.437
23	3.072	3.426	3.820	4.256	4.741	5.277	5.871
24	3.225	3.615	4.049	4.533	5.072	5.673	6.341
25	3.386	3.813	4.292	4.828	5.427	6.098	6.848
26	3.556	4.023	4.549	5.141	5.807	6.556	7.396
27	3.733	4.244	4.822	5.476	6.214	7.047	7.988
28	3.920	4.478	5.112	5.832	6.649	7.576	8.627
29	4.116	4.724	5.418	6.211	7.114	8.144	9.317
30	4.322	4.984	5.743	6.614	7.612	8.755	10.063
31	4.538	5.258	6.088	7.044	8.145	9.412	10.868
32	4.765	5.547	6.453	7.502	8.715	10.117	11.737
33	5.003	5.852	6.841	7.990	9.325	10.876	12.676
34	5.253	6.174	7.251	8.509	9.978	11.692	13.690
35	5.516	6.514	7.686	9.062	10.677	12.569	14.785
36	5.792	6.872	8.147	9.651	11.424	13.512	15.968
37	6.081	7.250	8.636	10.279	12.224	14.525	17.246
38	6.385	7.649	9.154	10.947	13.079	15.614	18.625
39	6.705	8.069	9.704	11.658	13.995	16.785	20.115
40	7.040	8.513	10.286	12.416	14.974	18.044	21.725
41	7.392	8.982	10.903	13.223	16.023	19.398	23.462
42	7.762	9.476	11.557	14.083	17.144	20.852	25.339

Factor = (1 + interest rate) to the power of the number of years can be written as: $(1+i)^n$.

APPENDIX 1–A(3)
Present Value of One Dollar Per Year

Years	.050	.055	.060	Interest Rates .065	.070	.075	.080
1	1.000	1.000	1.000	1.000	1.000	1.000	1.000
2	1.952	1.948	1.943	1.939	1.935	1.930	1.926
3	2.859	2.846	2.833	2.821	2.808	2.796	2.783
4	3.723	3.698	3.673	3.648	3.624	3.601	3.577
5	4.546	4.505	4.465	4.426	4.387	4.349	4.312
6	5.329	5.270	5.212	5.156	5.100	5.046	4.993
7	6.076	5.996	5.917	5.841	5.767	5.694	5.623
8	6.786	6.683	6.582	6.485	6.389	6.297	6.206
9	7.463	7.335	7.210	7.089	6.971	6.857	6.747
10	8.108	7.952	7.802	7.656	7.515	7.379	7.247
11	8.722	8.538	8.360	8.189	8.024	7.864	7.710
12	9.306	9.093	8.887	8.689	8.499	8.315	8.139
13	9.863	9.619	9.384	9.159	8.943	8.735	8.536
14	10.394	10.117	9.853	9.600	9.358	9.126	8.904
15	10.899	10.590	10.295	10.014	9.745	9.489	9.244
16	11.380	11.038	10.712	10.403	10.108	9.827	9.559
17	11.838	11.462	11.106	10.768	10.447	10.142	9.851
18	12.274	11.865	11.477	11.111	10.763	10.434	10.122
19	12.690	12.246	11.828	11.432	11.059	10.706	10.372
20	13.085	12.608	12.158	11.735	11.336	10.959	10.604

21	13.462	12.950	12.470	12.019	11.594	11.194	10.818
22	13.821	13.275	12.764	12.285	11.836	11.413	11.017
23	14.163	13.583	13.042	12.535	12.061	11.617	11.201
24	14.489	13.875	13.303	12.770	12.272	11.807	11.371
25	14.799	14.152	13.550	12.991	12.469	11.983	11.529
26	15.094	14.414	13.783	13.198	12.654	12.147	11.675
27	15.375	14.662	14.003	13.392	12.826	12.299	11.810
28	15.643	14.898	14.211	13.575	12.987	12.441	11.935
29	15.898	15.121	14.406	13.746	13.137	12.573	12.051
30	16.141	15.333	14.591	13.907	13.278	12.696	12.158
31	16.372	15.534	14.765	14.059	13.409	12.810	12.258
32	16.593	15.724	14.929	14.201	13.532	12.917	12.350
33	16.803	15.904	15.084	14.334	13.647	13.015	12.435
34	17.003	16.075	15.230	14.459	13.754	13.107	12.514
35	17.193	16.237	15.368	14.577	13.854	13.193	12.587
36	17.374	16.391	15.498	14.687	13.948	13.273	12.655
37	17.547	16.536	15.621	14.791	14.035	13.347	12.717
38	17.711	16.674	15.737	14.888	14.117	13.415	12.775
39	17.868	16.805	15.846	14.979	14.193	13.479	12.829
40	18.017	16.929	15.949	15.065	14.265	13.539	12.879
41	18.159	17.046	16.046	15.146	14.332	13.594	12.925
42	18.294	17.157	16.138	15.221	14.394	13.646	12.967

Factor = (1 − (1 + interest rate) to the negative power of the number divided by the interest rate, all times (interest rate + 1) can be written as: $\ddot{a}_{\overline{n}|i}$.

APPENDIX 1–A(4)
Accumulation of One Dollar Per Year

Years	Interest Rates						
	.050	.055	.060	.065	.070	.075	.080
1	1.050	1.055	1.060	1.065	1.070	1.075	1.080
2	2.153	2.168	2.184	2.199	2.215	2.231	2.246
3	3.310	3.342	3.375	3.407	3.440	3.473	3.506
4	4.526	4.581	4.637	4.694	4.751	4.808	4.867
5	5.802	5.888	5.975	6.064	6.153	6.244	6.336
6	7.142	7.267	7.394	7.523	7.654	7.787	7.923
7	8.549	8.722	8.897	9.077	9.260	9.446	9.637
8	10.027	10.256	10.491	10.732	10.978	11.230	11.488
9	11.578	11.875	12.181	12.494	12.816	13.147	13.487
10	13.207	13.583	13.972	14.372	14.784	15.208	15.645
11	14.917	15.386	15.870	16.371	16.888	17.424	17.977
12	16.713	17.287	17.882	18.500	19.141	19.806	20.495
13	18.599	19.293	20.015	20.767	21.550	22.366	23.215
14	20.579	21.409	22.276	23.182	24.129	25.118	26.152
15	22.657	23.641	24.673	25.754	26.888	28.077	29.324
16	24.840	25.996	27.213	28.493	29.840	31.258	32.750
17	27.132	28.481	29.906	31.410	32.999	34.677	36.450
18	29.539	31.103	32.760	34.517	36.379	38.353	40.446
19	32.066	33.868	35.786	37.825	39.995	42.305	44.762
20	34.719	36.786	38.993	41.349	43.865	46.553	49.423

21	37.505	39.864	42.392	45.102	48.006	51.119	-54.457
22	40.430	43.112	45.996	49.098	52.436	56.028	59.893
23	43.502	46.538	49.816	53.355	57.177	61.305	65.765
24	46.727	50.153	53.865	57.888	62.249	66.978	72.106
25	50.113	53.966	58.156	62.715	62.676	73.076	78.954
26	53.669	57.989	62.706	67.857	73.484	79.632	86.351
27	57.403	62.234	67.528	73.333	79.698	86.679	94.339
28	61.323	66.711	72.640	79.164	86.347	92.255	102.966
29	65.439	71.435	78.058	85.375	93.461	102.439	112.283
30	69.761	76.419	83.802	91.989	101.073	111.154	122.346
31	74,299	81.677	89.890	99.034	109.218	120.566	133.214
32	79.064	87.225	96.343	106.536	117.933	130.683	144.951
33	84.067	93.077	103.184	114.526	127.259	141.560	157.627
34	89.320	99.251	110.435	123.035	137.237	153.252	171.317
35	94.836	105.765	118.121	132.097	147.913	165.820	186.102
36	100.628	112.637	126.268	141.748	159.337	179.332	202.070
37	106.710	119.887	134.904	152.027	171.561	193.857	219.316
38	113.095	127.536	144.058	162.974	184.640	209.471	237.941
39	119.800	135.606	153.762	174.632	198.635	226.257	258.057
40	126.840	144.119	164.048	187.048	213.610	244.301	279.781
41	134.232	153.100	174.951	200.271	229.632	263.698	303.244
42	141.993	162.576	186.508	214.354	246.776	284.551	328.583

Factor = ((1 + interest rate) to the power of the number of years) divided by the interest rate, all times (interest rate + 1) can be written as: $\overline{S}_{\overline{n}|j}$.

APPENDIX 1–B
Commutation Functions for UP84 Unisex Mortality Table 6 × (1 year Setback)

Age X	DX	NX	CX	MX	DXS	NXS
25	2440296	39923813	2645.233	180457.545	2440296	39923813
26	2299521	37483517	2449.123	177812.311	2299521	37483517
27	2166910	35183996	2263.006	175363.188	2166910	35183996
28	2041992	33017086	2086.395	173100.181	2041992	33017086
29	1924321	30975094	1920.682	171013.786	1924321	30975094
30	1813476	29050773	1852.880	169093.104	1813476	29050773
31	1708974	27237296	1791.199	167240.224	1708974	27237296
32	1610448	25528322	1733.508	165449.025	1610448	25528322
33	1517557	23917874	1679.387	163715.517	1517557	23917874
34	1429979	22400317	1629.701	162036.129	1429979	22400317
35	1347407	20970338	1648.693	160406.429	1347407	20970338
36	1269490	19622931	1674.307	158757.735	1269490	19622931
37	1195957	18353442	1707.023	157083.428	1195957	18353442
38	1126555	17157484	1746.183	155376.405	1126555	17157484
39	1061041	16030929	1793.784	153630.222	1061041	16030929
40	999189	14969888	1836.235	151836.438	999189	14969888
41	940795	13970699	1965.906	150000.203	940795	13970699
42	885576	13029905	1944.098	148034.297	885576	13029905
43	833505	12144329	2009.885	146090.199	833505	12144329
44	784316	11310824	2085.098	144080.314	784316	11310824
45	737835	10526508	2154.365	141995.216	737835	10526508
46	693917	9788673	2232.345	139840.851	693917	9788673
47	652406	9094756	2319.746	137608.506	652406	9094756
48	613158	8442350	2417.916	135288.760	613158	8442350

49	576033	7829193	132870.844	2518.774	576033	7829193
50	540908	7253160	130352.071	2603.996	540908	7253160
51	507687	6712252	127748.075	2689.783	507687	6712252
52	476260	6204565	125058.292	2783.897	476260	6204565
53	446518	5728305	122274.395	2886.771	446518	5728305
54	418357	5281787	119387.624	2977.035	418357	5281787
55	391699	4863430	116410.589	3058.946	391699	4863430
56	366468	4471731	113351.643	3122.926	366468	4471731
57	342602	4105262	110228.717	3191.706	342602	4105262
58	320018	3762660	107037.011	3264.799	320018	3762660
59	298639	3442643	103772.212	3342.206	298639	3442643
60	278392	3144004	100430.006	3401.632	278392	3144004
61	259233	2865611	97028.374	3463.442	259233	2865611
62	241096	2606378	93564.932	3527.509	241096	2606378
63	223921	2365283	90037.423	3593.308	223921	2365283
64	207653	2141361	86444.115	3660.382	207653	2141361
65	192239	1933708	82783.733	3720.899	192239	1933708
66	177637	1741469	79062.834	3780.981	177637	1741469
67	163801	1563833	75281.852	3839.578	163801	1563833
68	150689	1400032	71442.275	3871.285	150689	1400032
69	138288	1249343	67570.989	3866.073	138288	1249343
70	126595	1111054	63704.917	3830.443	126595	1111054

The formula to calculate the annuity purchase rate for an annuity paid monthly is as follows:

$$\ddot{a}_y^{(m)} \doteq \frac{N_x - \left(\frac{m-1}{2m}\right) D_x}{D_x}.$$

Therefore, the annuity purchase rate used was calculated as follows:
(((1,933,708 − (11/24 × 192,239)) / 192,239)) × 12 = 115.2064956. This number was rounded to 115.21.

APPENDIX 2

REVIEW OF FINANCIAL CALCULATIONS

Interest: The fact that money invested is expected to earn additional money is at the heart of financial calculations. When money is invested, an institution of some sort is using that money. The money paid for the use of money is called *interest.* Generally, interest is compounded, meaning the interest earned is also earning interest as time passes.

Accumulated Value of Money: The accumulated value of money is the original value plus the interest earned during the period involved.

Present Value of Money: The present value of money is also known as the discounted value of money. It is the converse of the accumulated value of money. The present value of a sum of money is its equivalent value at an earlier date. In other words, it is the amount of money that must be accumulated over time, with interest, to yield a specific amount at the end of the time period.

SYMBOLS

Accumulated value is sometimes denoted by S.
Present value is denoted by A or v.
Time is denoted by n.
Interest rate is denoted by i.

CALCULATIONS

Accumulated value is $(1 + i)^n$.
Present value is $1 / (1 + i)^n$ or $(1 + i)^{-n}$.

Annuities Certain: A sequence of payments made at regular intervals over a certain period is known as an annuity certain. An immediate annuity is due at the end of each regular interval, and an annuity due is due at the beginning of each regular interval. Both accumulated and present values can be calculated for annuities certain.

SYMBOLS

Accumulated value of an annuity certain is denoted by $s_{\overline{n}|i}$.
Present value of an annuity certain is denoted by $a_{\overline{n}|i}$.
(For annuities due, double dots are placed over the s or a

$$\ddot{s}_{\overline{n}|i}$$
$$\ddot{a}_{\overline{n}|i}).$$

CALCULATIONS

Accumulated value of an annuity certain is $\dfrac{(1 + i)^n - 1}{i}$.

Present value of an annuity certain is $\dfrac{1 - (1 + i)^{-n}}{i}$.

(For annuities due, multiply the factor obtained by the above formulas by the interest rate.)

$$\ddot{a}_{\overline{n}|i} = a_{\overline{n}|i} \, x \, (1 + i).$$
$$\ddot{s}_{\overline{n}|i} = s_{\overline{n}|i} \, x \, (1 + i).$$

The interest tables found in Appendix 1 were generated using these formulas.

APPENDIX 3

DEFINITIONS OF COMMON ACTUARIAL SYMBOLS AND DERIVATIONS OF COMMUTATION FACTORS FOR THE BEGINNER

Many symbols are used in actuarial science. This appendix is not a thorough discussion of the meaning, use, and derivation of these symbols; it is only a review of the basics.

Note, the x in each symbol denotes an age. An n denotes a number of years.

1. l_x : Number of people living at age x. For example, according to the 1958 C.S.O. Mortality Table, there are 9,929,200 people living at age 1. The table begins at age 0 with 10,000,000 people.

2. d_x: Number of people dying between age x and age $(x + 1)$. Therefore, d_x at age 0 in the above example is 70,800.

3. q_x: Probability of dying at a certain age. The formula is: $d_x / l_x = q_x$.

4. p_x: Probability of living to the next age. The formula is: $l_{x+1} / l_x = p_x$.

5. $_np_x$: Probability of living from a certain age for a given number of years. The formula is: $l_{x+n} / l_x = {_np_x}$.

6. Life annuity: An annuity payment made only if the person is alive. Uses both life contingency and interest concepts. For example, the formula for a whole life annuity of $1 beginning at age 90 is:

$$\frac{l_{91}v + l_{92}v^2 + l_{93}v^3 \ldots \text{to end of mortality table}}{l_{90}}.$$

7. Commutation factors: Make calculation of life annuities simpler by use of tables.

$D_x = 1_x v^x$.

$N_x = (D_x + D_{x+1} + D_{x+2} + \ldots$ to end of mortality table).

8. Calculation of the present value of various types of annuities using commutation factors:

Whole life annuity $= a_x = \dfrac{N_{x+1}}{D_x}$.

Whole life annuity due $= \ddot{a}_x = \dfrac{N_x}{D_x}$.

Temporary life annuity for n years $= a_{x:\overline{n}|} = \dfrac{N_{x+1} - N_{x+n+1}}{D_x}$.

Whole life annuity, deferred for m years $= {}_{m|}a_x = \dfrac{N_{x+m+1}}{D_x}$.

Whole life annuity due, deferred for m years $= {}_{m|}\ddot{a}_x = \dfrac{N_{x+m}}{D_x}$.

Temporary life annuity for n years, deferred for m years $=$

${}_{m|}a_{x\overline{n}|} = \dfrac{N_{x+m+1} - N_{x+m+n+1}}{D_x}$.

Temporary life annuity due for n years, deferred for m years $=$

${}_{m|}\ddot{a}_{x\overline{n}|} = \dfrac{N_{x+m} - N_{x+m+n}}{D_x}$.

Adjustments are made if the payments are more often than once a year. The adjustment is $-(\dfrac{m-1}{2m})D_x$ where m is the number of periods during the year. For example, as shown in Appendix 1–B, the formula for an annuity paid monthly for life is:

$$\ddot{a}_x^{(m)} \doteqdot \dfrac{N_x - (\dfrac{m-1}{2m})D_x}{D_x}.$$

ANSWERS TO STUDY PROBLEMS

CHAPTER 3

1. The annuity purchase rates are the same because the normal retirement age is the same. Additionally, the annuity purchase rate is the same regardless of the sex of the participant because a unisex mortality table is being used.
2. The annuity purchase rates would differ if the normal retirement ages differed. Some plans have a normal retirement age such as the later of age 65 or 10 years of plan participation. The annuity purchase rates would also differ for males and females if a unisex mortality table were not used.
3. There is no past service liability because the normal cost is calculated as of the date of participation or the date of increase in benefits, not as of the date of employment.
4. The normal cost would be $3,940, calculated as follows:

    $32,000 \times 0.50 / 12 \times 115.21 / 38.993 = \$3,940$ (rounded).

CHAPTER 4

1. Step 1: Calculate present value of future benefits.

    Participant 1: $192,055 \times 0.55839 = \$107,242$.
    Participant 2: $72,009 \times 0.13011 = \$9,369$.
    Total = $116,611.

    Step 2: Calculate present value of future normal costs.

    Participant 1: $3,302 \times 7.802 = \$25,762$
    Participant 2: $439 \times 15.368 = \$6,747$.
    Total = $32,509.

    Step 3: Calculate past service liability.

    $116,611 - 32,509 = \$84,102$.

2. Under the individual level premium funding method, the normal costs are calculated as of the date they first arise, initially with the date of participation. If changes to the benefit occur due to salary changes, they are treated as additional benefits and are funded beginning on the date of the change. Therefore, different accumulation factors are used as the participant gets nearer to retirement.

   Under the entry age normal funding method, normal costs are always calculated as of the entry date (usually defined as the date of hire) and, therefore, the same accumulation factor is always used.

3. The normal cost would be $3,624, calculated as follows:

   $32,000 × 0.50 / 12 × 115.21 / 42.392 = $3,624 (rounded).

4. Since the participant with the highest benefits is only 10 years from retirement, the plan runs the danger of not accumulating enough money to pay benefits. This could easily happen if the minimum contribution is usually made.

CHAPTER 5

1. If you understand present value/future value relationships, you find that you are doing the same calculation from different points in time. Under the individual level premium funding method, we projected to the future and determined the amount to contribute each year to obtain that amount. Under the individual spread gain funding method, we determined the value now of a future benefit and amortized it. Either calculation could be used for the first year under either funding method.

2. The accrued liability would equal the assets under the individual spread gain funding method. Therefore, the unfunded liability would always be zero, since the unfunded liability is defined as the accrued liability − assets.

3. The significance of Problem 2 is that there is no need to calculate actuarial gains or losses separately because they are automatically part of the normal cost. This leads to the name of this funding method, individual *spread gain*.

CHAPTER 6

1. The average temporary annuity would be the average of all participant's applicable factors from the present value of one dollar per year

table in the appendixes. You would not multiply by salary, since salaries have no effect on the benefit.

2. The trust assets are available to pay future benefits. Therefore, it is not necessary to make a contribution for the benefits that are already covered by plan assets.

3. The present value of benefits for Participant 4 was calculated as follows: $28,000 \times 0.50 / 12 \times 115.21 \times 0.2168 = \$29,140$.

   The present value of future salaries for Participant 4 was calculated as follows:

$$\$28,000 \times 13.042 = \$365,176.$$
$$\text{The total present value of benefits} = \$29,140 + \$116,612$$
$$= \$145,752.$$
$$\text{The present value of future salaries} = \$365,176 + \$542,600$$
$$= \$907,776.$$
$$\text{The average temporary annuity} = \$907,776 / \$83,000$$
$$= 10.937.$$
$$\text{Normal cost} = \$145,752 / 10.937$$
$$= \$13,327.$$

CHAPTER 7

1. The unfunded past service liability would not be subtracted from the present value of future benefits when calculating the normal cost. The frozen initial funding method would become the aggregate funding method.

2. Step 1: $32,000 \times 0.50 / 12 \times 115.21 \times 0.3118 = \$47,897 =$ present value of benefits. Added to the other participants' present value of benefits $= \$47,897 + \$116,611 = \$164,508 =$ Total present value of benefits.

   Step 2: $32,000 \times 12.158 = \$389,056 =$ present value of future salaries. Added to the other participants' present value of future salaries $= \$389,056 + 542,600 = \$931,656 =$ Total present value of future salaries.

   Step 3: Past service liability for Participant 3 $= \$3,624 \times 1.06 = \$3,841$. This is the entry age normal cost accumulated for one year. Add this to the other participants' past service liability $= \$3,841 + 84,093 = \$87,934$.

   Step 4: $931,656 / 87,000 = 10.70869 =$ Average temporary annuity factor.

   Step 5: $(\$164,508 - 87,934 - 0) / 10.70869 = \$7,151 =$ Normal cost.

CHAPTER 8

1. The second year normal cost is 1.06 times the first year normal cost. The benefit accruing during the year stayed the same over the two years. Therefore, the plan is funding for the same benefit, only it is doing so one year later. Since our interest assumption is six percent, the second year contribution must be 1.06 times the first year contribution. Assuming no changes in the benefit accruing during the year, each year's normal cost would be 1.06 times the prior year's normal cost. This fact would not hold true if a mortality or turnover assumption is used. (See Chapter 10.)
2. Under the current example, the benefit is not tied to salary. Therefore, the salary increase in the second year made no difference in the benefit being funded.
3. There was an actuarial gain, not an actuarial loss. Therefore, the plan had more money than expected, and so future contributions can be less.

CHAPTER 9

1. As given in the chapter, the accrued benefit is $483 and the benefit accruing during the year is $97. To determine the accrued liability, we multiply the accrued benefit times the annuity purchase rate and the present value of one dollar factor. Since we are told the participant has five years until retirement, we use the present value factor for five years. To determine the normal cost, we multiply the benefit accruing during the year times the annuity purchase rate and the present value of one dollar factor for five years. The calculations are as follows:

   Accrued liability = $483 × 115.21 × .74726 = $41,582.
   Normal cost = $97 × 115.21 × .74726 = $8,351.

2. Using the participant data found in Chapter 7, we calculate the accrued benefit past service liability. The first step is to calculate the accrued benefit for each participant.

   Participant 1: Monthly benefit = $1,667.
   Accrued benefit = $1,667 × 15/25 = $1,000.

   (The accrual fraction = 15 years of service so far divided by 25 possible years of service to normal retirement age.)

Past service liability $= \$1,000 \times 115.21 \times .55839$
$= \$64,332.$
Participant 2: Monthly benefit $= \$625.$
Accrued benefit $= \$625 \times 5/40 = \$78.$

(The accrual fraction $= 5$ years of service so far divided by 40 possible years of service to normal retirement age.)

Past service liability $= \$78 \times 115.21 \times .13011 = \$1,169.$
Total past service liability $= \$64,332 + 1,169 = \$65,501.$

In Chapter 7, we can find the components needed to calculate the normal cost.

Present value of future benefits $= \$116,611.$
Present value of future salaries $= \$542,600.$
Salaries $= \$55,000.$
Average temporary annuity $= \$542,600 / 55,000 = 9.8655.$
Normal cost $=$ (Present value of benefits $-$
Unfunded past service liability $-$
Trust assets) / Average temporary
annuity
$=$ ($\$116,611 - 65,501 - 0$)
$/ 9.8655$
$= \$5,181.$

3. The following information from the second plan year can be taken from Chapter 3:

Accrued liability $= \$15,206.$
Expected unfunded liability $= (895).$

Calculate the Unfunded liability $=$ Accrued liability $-$ Assets, including the Cash value $= \$15,206 - 17,000 = \$(1,794).$
Calculate the Actuarial gain or loss $=$ Expected unfunded liability $-$
Actual unfunded liability $= \$(895) - 0 = \$(895).$

INDEX